BLITZ CATALOGING WORKBOOK

MARC/AACR2/ Authority Control Tagging

Other Blitz Cataloging Workbooks

Cataloging Nonprint Materials
Subject Analysis

BLITZ CATALOGING WORKBOOK

MARC/AACR2/ Authority Control Tagging

Bobby Ferguson

1998
Libraries Unlimited, Inc.
Englewood, Colorado

LIBRARIES UNLIMITED, INC.
P.O. Box 6633
Englewood, CO 80155-6633
(800) 237-6124
www.lu.com

Constance Hardesty, *Project Manager*
Brooke Graves, *Editor*
Sheryl Tongue, *Design and Composition*

Library of Congress Cataloging-in-Publication Data

Ferguson, Anna S.
MARC/AACR2/authority control tagging : blitz cataloging workbook / Bobby Ferguson
xi, 175 p. 22×28 cm.
Includes bibliographical references (p. 129).
ISBN 1-56308-644-1 (pbk.)
1. Authority files (Information retrieval)--United States.
2. Authority files (Information retrieval)--United States--Data processing.
3. Anglo-American cataloguing rules. 4. MARC formats--United States.
5. Descriptive cataloging--United States--Rules. I. Title
Z693.3.A88F47 1998
025.3'2--dc21 98-2811
CIP

Table of Contents

Acknowledgments

I would like to express my appreciation and gratitude to Tom Jaques, Mickey McKann, and Elisabeth Spanhoff of the State Library of Louisiana; Anna Marchiafava of the West Baton Rouge Parish Library; all the Sharps and Fergusons; Ajaye Bloomstone, Sandy Colby, and Terre Ferguson; Gary Ferguson for help with the wording and proofing, and for his continuing friendship; and my editor, Sheila Intner, for all her help, friendship, and knowledge. Thank you all.

BLITZ CATALOGING WORKBOOK SERIES

Introduction

Cataloging and classification are the most important parts of librarianship. Without a catalog, either manual or electronic, a library is no more than a room full of books and cannot provide services to its patrons in a reliable, timely fashion. Other library activities, such as acquisition of new materials, interlibrary lending, and reference, cannot be accomplished if patrons and staff cannot find out what a particular library contains.

Knowledge of cataloging is important to all librarians, not just catalogers. As more and more libraries become automated, a knowledge of MARC fields and electronic formats, as well as call numbers and subject headings, is essential and will make all librarians more proficient. Using these workbooks should cause you to absorb a lot of information that will be useful to you in any library situation.

As for catalogers, you will find that you cannot do a superior job as a beginning cataloger. Experience is necessary, preferably under an experienced cataloger. These workbooks are intended to reinforce your knowledge of the fundamentals of cataloging. They will help you to understand the MARC format and functions of the various fields and subfields; to evaluate copy cataloging and classification of various formats of materials; to locate errors and inconsistencies; to learn access points and which are the most important; to assign subject headings using both *Library of Congress Subject Headings* and *Sears List of Subject Headings*; to assign call numbers in both Dewey and LC classification schedules; and to evaluate and construct cross-references and authority headings.

DESCRIPTIVE CATALOGING

Introduction

Cataloging in an online environment follows two basic sets of rules: *Anglo-American Cataloguing Rules*, 2nd edition, 1988 revision, called *AACR2R*, and the Machine Readable Cataloging format, or MARC. *AACR2R* is, of course, the more important of the two, and takes precedence over the MARC format where there are inconsistencies.

MARC was designed to make cataloging usable by computers. Some difficulties are caused by the programming of individual integrated library systems such as NOTIS, Galaxy, Innovation Access, Dynix, and CLSI. For example, *AACR2R* gives rules for notes that require 5xx fields to be entered in a particular order, but not the MARC format's numerical order. Some systems automatically line the fields up in numerical order, thus forcing the MARC cataloging record to take precedence over *AACR2R*. When this happens, the cataloger's hands are tied—there is no way the proper order can be applied. In this workbook the integrated library system will be designed correctly, and *AACR2R* will always take precedence over the MARC format.

British spellings and terminology were adopted in the text of *AACR2*. There will, therefore, be what appear to be inconsistent spellings in the text.

This workbook is designed to help you learn the correct way of applying cataloging tools, identifying errors in both original and copy cataloging, and maintaining proper authority control for more complete access.

1.
MARC FORMAT

Introduction

A knowledge of tags, indicators, fields, and subfields is essential for all catalogers and, indeed, all librarians. The numeric tags tell in computer-recognizable language what information is contained in the ensuing field. Reference librarians will find this helpful in decoding the record. For catalogers, this knowledge is the most important part of automated cataloging. Although *Anglo-American Cataloguing Rules* is the primary tool of original catalogers, knowledge of the computer format is essential for accurate inputting and retrieval of information from bibliographic records.

Indicators are digits found immediately following the three-digit field which "indicate" something to the computer. The chart beginning on page 17 gives the indicators for most fields, and will be useful in the tagging exercises.

Subfields are identified by letters or digits; ***a***, ***b***, and ***c*** are the most commonly used delimiters, and their meaning is field-specific. For instance, in the 245 field (title), ***a*** indicates the main title, ***b*** the subtitle, and ***c*** the statement of responsibility. In the 260 field (imprint), ***a*** indicates the place of publication, ***b*** the publisher or distributor, and ***c*** the date of publication. You will need to use the *USMARC Bibliographic Format* to help you with the tagging exercises.

Authority control has its own MARC format. The tags and subfields are different from the bibliographic MARC record, and the relationship between the tags is different. Because of this, a separate section on authority control is included in section 3 of this volume.

1.1. Families of Tags

Different tags that begin with the same digit form a group, or family, of tags and are referred to by the first digit(s) followed by "xx" or "x". These families are briefly explained below, followed by exercises.

0xx Primarily coded data to help the computer better utilize information. Usually only a cataloger will understand and/or use this data.

1xx Main entry fields. This may be a personal name, a corporate name, a conference, meeting or event name, or a uniform title.

24x Title fields. This may include a uniform title, a main title, or added titles.

25x Edition and scale fields.

260 Imprint. This is not a family, as there is only one 26x field in a record.

3xx Physical description. Also includes frequency, publication dates, and/or volume designations for serials.

4xx Series. These may be title or author/title entries, traced or untraced.

5xx Notes. There are many types of notes. They include bibliographies, contents, summaries, cast or credits, dissertations, and many more, including general notes, which may be anything the cataloger wants to add.

6xx Subjects. These are personal or corporate names, conferences or events, topics, geographic names, or uniform titles.

7xx Added entries. These may include, among others, joint authors; illustrators or editors; corporate bodies; analytical entries; or linking entries.

8xx Added series entries and other linking entries.

9xx Local fields. These give library-specific information and may be defined as libraries wish. They may include accession numbers, copy numbers, branch locations, donor information for gifts, date of cataloging, bindery information, or anything else a library wishes to include in the records.

Some data elements dealing with types of names can be found in more than one field. These are assigned two-digit codes which are added to the first digit of the field in which they appear. Each of these families of tags is designated by an "x" followed by the two-digit code.

x00 Personal names. These may be found as main entries (100), series entries (400/800), subjects (600), or added entries (700).

x10 Corporate names.

x11 Conference or meeting names.

x30 Uniform titles.

Families of Tags Exercises

Write the tag family on the blank before each of the following types of bibliographic data.

1.1.1. ________________ Subjects

1.1.2. ________________ Imprint

1.1.3. ________________ Series

1.1.4. ______________ Local fields

1.1.5. ______________ Main entry

1.1.6. ______________ Computer utilization fields

1.1.7. ______________ Added series

1.1.8. ______________ Physical description

1.1.9. ______________ Added entries

1.1.10. ______________ Title fields

1.1.11. ______________ Edition and scale fields

1.1.12. ______________ Notes fields

Write the names of the tag families on the line following the tag.

1.1.13. 9xx ______________________________

1.1.14. 0xx ______________________________

1.1.15. 7xx ______________________________

1.1.16. 24x ______________________________

1.1.17. 5xx ______________________________

1.1.18. 1xx ______________________________

1.1.19. 8xx ______________________________

1.1.20. 25x ______________________________

1.1.21. 3xx ______________________________

1.1.22. 6xx ______________________________

1.1.23. 4xx ______________________________

1.1.24. 260 ______________________________

Write the names of the data elements on the blank following each tag.

1.1.25. x30 ______________________________

1.1.26. x00 ______________________________

1.1.27. x11 ______________________________

1.1.28. x10 ______________________________

Write the tags on the line preceding the names of the data elements.

1.1.29. ______________ Uniform titles

1.1.30. ______________ Corporate names

1.1.31. ______________ Conference or meeting names

1.1.32. ______________ Personal names

1.2. 008 (Header) Information, Bibliographic Records

The header in bibliographic and authority records is used to record the basic information such as the date the record was created, whether the work is juvenile, fiction, or biographical, or whether it is a government document. This information is given in field 008 and consists of forty character positions numbered 00–39, which contain defined data elements and provide coded information about the record as a whole or about special format aspects of the item being cataloged. Some indexing information is taken from the 008 field rather than the textual fields in the body of the record. Character positions 00–17 and 35–39 are the same for all formats; positions 18–34 are different for each format, with some exceptions. A data element common to more than one format always occupies the same character position in the record. For example, whenever a format has an element defined as **Government publication**, the element is in position 28. The Music format, for example, has no **Government publication** element, so position 28 is used for something else. The Maps format, on the other hand, does have a **Government publication** element, which is in position 28. Positions 26–27 and 29–30 are currently undefined.

Undefined character positions contain either a blank or a fill character (|). Each defined character position must contain either a defined code or a fill character. The characters defined across all formats (positions 00–17 and 35–39), as well as positions 18–34 for books, are given here. All codes (Country of publication code, Language code, and others) are taken from USMARC code lists.

The following lists identify the 40 character positions for the 008 field. The first list identifies character positions used for all materials, regardless of type; the second list identifies the character positions used when cataloging books.

008—All Materials

00–05 Date entered on file; indicates the date the record was created; recorded in the pattern *yymmdd* (year/year/month/month/day/day).

06 Type of date/publication status. One-character code that categorizes the type of dates given in 008/07–10 (Date 1) and 008/11–14 (Date 2). For serials, 008/06 also indicates the publication status.

b—No dates given; B.C. date involved. Each character in fields 008/07–10 and 008/11–14 contains a blank.

c—Serial item currently published. 008/07–10 contains the beginning date of publication; 008/11–14 contains 9999.

d—Serial item ceased publication. 008/07–10 contains beginning date of publication, 008/11–14 contains ending date.

e—Detailed date; 008/07–10 contains year and 008/11–14 contains month and day, recorded as *mmdd.*

i—Inclusive dates of collection.

k—Range of years of bulk of collection.

m—Multiple dates; 008/07–10 usually contains the beginning date and 008/11–14 contains the ending date.

n—Dates unknown; each position in 008/07–10 and 008/11–14 contain blanks.

p—Date of distribution/release/issue and production/recording session when different.

q—Questionable date; 008/07–10 contains the earliest possible date; 008/11–14 contains the latest possible date.

r—Reprint/reissue date and original date; 008/07–10 contains the date of reproduction or reissue (i.e., the most current date) and 008/11–14 contains the date of the original, if known.

s—Single known/probable date. 008/07–10 contains the date; 008/11–14 contains blanks.

t—Publication date and copyright date.

u—Serial status unknown. 008/07–10 contains the beginning date of publication; 008/11–14 contains 9999.

07–10 (Date 1)

(blank)—Date element is not applicable.

u—Elements of date which are partially unknown. *[197u; 18uu]*

nnnn—Four-digit date of publication, or beginning date of publication.

11–14 (Date 2)

(blank)—Date element is not applicable.

u—Elements of date which are totally or partially unknown.

nnnn—Ending date of publication.

15–17 Place of publication, production, or execution. A two- or three-character code that indicates the place of publication, production, or execution. Two-character codes are left-justified and the unused position contains a blank. [Codes for the United States consist of the two-letter ZIP code abbreviation plus u for United States. New York, for example, would be coded nyu.] Unless otherwise specified, codes are always lower-case letters.

35–37 Language. A three-character code indicating the language of the item.

38 Modified record. A one-character code that indicates whether any data in a bibliographic record is a modification of information that appeared on the item being cataloged or that was intended to be included in the USMARC record. Codes are assigned a priority and, when more than one code applies to the item, are recorded in the order of the following list.

- (blank)—Not modified.
- d—Dashed-on information.
- o—Completely romanized/printed in script.
- s—Shortened. Some data omitted because the record would have exceeded the maximum length allowed by a particular system.
- x—Missing characters. Characters could not be converted into machine-readable form due to character-set limitations.

39 Cataloging source. A one-character code that indicates the creator of the original cataloging record. The NUC symbol or the name of the organization may be contained in subfield ≠a of field 040.

- (blank)—Library of Congress
- a—National Agricultural Library
- b—National Library of Medicine
- c—Library of Congress cooperative cataloging program
- d—Other sources [most libraries fall here]
- n—Report to *New Serial Titles*
- u—Unknown

008—Books

18–21 Illustrations. Up to four one-character codes recorded in alphabetical order that indicate the presence of types of illustrations in the item. Codes are left-justified and each unused position contains a blank.

- (blank)—No illustrations
- a—Illustrations
- b—Maps
- c—Portraits
- d—Charts
- e—Plans
- f—Plates
- g—Music
- h—Facsimiles
- i—Coats of arms
- j—Genealogical tables
- k—Forms
- l—Samples
- m—Phonodisc, phonowire
- o—Photographs
- p—Illuminations

22 Target audience
(blank)—Unknown or not specified
a—Preschool
b—Primary
c—Elementary and junior high school
d—Secondary (senior high school)
e—Adult
f—Specialized
g—General
j—Juvenile

23 Form of item
(blank)—None of the following
a—Microfilm
b—Microfiche
c—Microopaque
d—Large print
f—Braille
r—Regular print reproduction; eye-readable print

24–27 Nature of contents. Up to four one-character codes recorded in alphabetical order that indicate whether a significant part of the item is, or contains, certain types of material. Codes are left-justified and the unused positions contain blanks.
(blank)—No specified nature of contents
a—Abstracts or summaries
b—Bibliographies
c—Catalogs
d—Dictionaries. Also glossaries or gazetteers
g—Legal articles
h—Handbooks
i—Indexes. Item is or contains an index to material *other* than itself
j—Patent document
k—Discographies
l—Legislation. Contains full or partial texts of enactments of legislative bodies or texts of rules and regulations issued by executive or administrative agencies
n—Surveys of literature in a subject area
p—Programmed texts
q—Filmographies
r—Directories
s—Statistics
t—Technical reports
v—Legal cases and case notes
w—Law reports and digests

28 Government publication. A one-character code indicating whether the item is published or produced by or for a government agency, and if so, the jurisdictional level of the agency.
(blank)—Not a government publication
a—Autonomous or semi-autonomous component
c—Multilocal
f—Federal/national
i—International/intergovernmental
l—Local
m—Multistate
o—Government publication—level undetermined
s—State, provincial, territorial, dependent, etc.
u—Unknown if item is government publication or not
z—Other
29 Conference publication
0—Not a conference publication
1—Conference publication
30 Festschrift
0—Not a festschrift
1—Festschrift
31 Index *[contains index to its own contents]*
0—No index
1—Index present
32 Undefined. Contains a blank (_) or fill character (|)
33 Fiction
0—Not fiction
1—Fiction
34 Biography
(blank)—No biographical/autobiographical material
a—Autobiography
b—Individual biography
c—Collective biography
d—Contains biographies

008 Field, Bibliographic Records, Exercise Set 1

1.2.1. Code the following dates in *yymmdd* format.

a. June 29, 1944 ____________________

b. May 1, 1986 ____________________

c. November 11, 1964 ____________________

d. April 15, 1989 ________________

e. September 23, 1996 ________________

f. March 8, 1978 ________________

1.2.2. Write the type of date, date 1, and date 2 on the appropriate lines.

a. Published in 1991, reprinted in 1997

___ ________ _______

b. Three volumes published between 1981 and 1987

___ ________ _______

c. Work published for the first time in 1997

___ ________ _______

d. Ongoing monographic series beginning in 1963

___ ________ _______

e. Published sometime in the 1970s

___ ________ _______

f. Probably published in the first half of the century

___ ________ _______

g. Produced in 1973, released in 1986

___ ________ _______

h. No indication of publishing date

___ ________ _______

1.2.3. Give the code for the place of publication. You will need the *USMARC Code List for Countries* to complete this section.

a. Missouri _______

b. New Jersey _______

c. Arkansas ________

d. Maryland ________

e. Massachusetts ________

f. Florida ________

g. England ________

h. France ________

i. China ________

j. Vietnam ________

k. Bosnia ________

1.2.4. Code for the following illustrations. Remember, the codes are recorded in alphabetical order.

a. Plates, genealogical tables, maps

____

b. Charts, photographs, music, plans, portraits

____

c. Pictures

____

d. Coats of arms, genealogical tables, facsimiles, forms

____

e. Samples, forms, plans, pictures

____

f. Music, phonodiscs, pictures

____

g. Maps, plans, charts

____

h. Illustrations, plates, portraits, facsimiles, illuminations

____

i. Portraits, illuminations, genealogical tables

____

j. Music, maps, charts

____

1.2.5. Code for the following audience levels.

a. Juvenile fiction ________

b. "Ages 5-7" ________

c. Ages 15 and up ________

d. Adult ________

e. For nurses ________

f. Preschool ________

g. High school ________

h. All ages ________

i. "Grades 4-8" ________

j. "Ages 5-9" ________

1.2.6. Code for the form of the item or work.

a. Microfiche ________

b. Braille ________

c. Microfilm ________

d. Large print ________

e. Microopaque ________

1.2.7. Code for the nature of contents.

a. Periodical index ________

b. Discography ________

c. Catalog of catalogs ________

d. Statistics ________

e. Legislation ________

f. Legal cases ________

g. Patent document ________

h. Bibliography ________

1.2.8. Code for the type of government publication.

a. Local ________

b. Federal ________

c. State ________

d. International ________

e. Not governmental ________

f. Multilocal ________

g. Multistate ________

1.2.9. Code for biography.

a. Autobiography ________

b. Collected biography ________

c. Collected autobiography ________

d. Biography ________

e. Contains biographical information ________

f. Contains no biographical information ________

1.2.10. Code for the language of the publication. You will need to use the *USMARC Code List for Languages.*

a. French ________

b. Vietnamese ________

c. English ________

d. Chinese ________

e. Spanish ________

f. German ________

g. Italian ________

h. Arabic ________

1.2.11. Code for type of modified record.

a. Shortened record ________

b. Dashed-on information ________

c. Missing characters ________

d. Romanized script ________

e. Unmodified record ________

1.2.12. Code for cataloging source.

a. Your library ________

b. Library of Congress ________

c. Report to *NST* ________

d. Simmons College ______

e. National Library of Medicine ______

f. Southern University ______

g. National Agricultural Library ______

h. Harvard University ______

1.2.13. Define the following positions. Identify each as G for general (i.e., for all materials) or M for monographs.

a. 008/06 ______

b. 008/30 ______

c. 008/15-17 ______

d. 008/29 ______

e. 008/00-05 ______

f. 008/35-37 ______

g. 008/18-21 ______

h. 008/39 ______

i. 008/24-27 ______

j. 008/07-10 ______

k. 008/32 ______

l. 008/38 ______

m. 008/11-14 ______

n. 008/31 ______

o. 008/28 ______

p. 008/22 ______

q. 008/34 ______________________

r. 008/23 ______________________

s. 008/33 ______________________

008 Field, Bibliographic Records, Exercise Set 2

In the following exercises you are given all the information you need to code the 008 field. Be careful of your spacing, and make sure your codes occupy the correct positions. Dots are given for help in identifying character positions.

1.2.14. 008 . . . .
100 1 ≠a Stringer, Chris.
245 10 ≠a African exodus : ≠b the origins of modern humanity.
250 ≠a 1st ed.
260 ≠a New York : ≠b Henry Holt, ≠c c1996.
300 ≠a xx, 282 p. : ≠b ill. ;≠c 25 cm.
504 ≠a Includes bibliographical references and index.

1.2.15. 008 . . . .
100 1 ≠a Gorman, Jacquelin.
245 14 ≠a The seeing glass: a memoir.
260 ≠a New York : ≠b Riverhead Books, ≠c 1997.
300 ≠a 255 p. ; ≠c 22 cm.

1.2.16. 008 . . . .
100 1 ≠a Stillman, Jackie.
245 14 ≠a The new Americans : ≠b how immigrants renew our country.
260 ≠a Starkville, Miss. : ≠b University of Mississippi, ≠c 1994.
300 ≠a x, 369 p. : ≠b ill., maps ; ≠c 25 cm.
504 ≠a Includes bibliographical references and index.

1.2.17. 008 . . . .
100 1 ≠a Mayer, Sharon.
245 10 ≠a Declaration of Independence, the American scripture.
260 ≠a New York : ≠b Frolic Press, ≠c 1995.
300 ≠a xxi, 300 p. : ≠b maps ; ≠c 25 cm.
500 ≠a Includes index.

1.2.18. 008 . . . .
100 1 ≠a Rogers, Elaine.
245 10 ≠a History of America's murders.
260 ≠a Columbus, Ohio : ≠b Field Press, ≠c 1996.
300 ≠a ix, 399 p., [8] p. of plates : ≠b ill., ports. ; ≠c 24 cm.
504 ≠a Includes bibliographical references (p. 355-387).

1.2.19. 008 . . . .
100 1 ≠a Thorne, John B.
245 12 ≠a L'histoire de la Louisiane.
250 ≠a 1st ed.
260 ≠a Paris : ≠b L'editions Francaise, ≠c 1997.
300 ≠a xx, 390 p. : ≠b ill. (some col.), maps ; ≠c 29 cm.
504 ≠a Includes bibliographical references and index.

1.2.20. 008 . . . .
100 1 ≠a Springer, Joshua.
245 10 ≠a Dinosaurs : ≠b everything too aged.
250 ≠a 6th ed.
260 ≠a Provo, Utah : ≠b Mormon Press, ≠c 1993.
300 ≠a 63 p. : ≠b col. ill., col. maps ; ≠c 24 cm.
500 ≠a Includes index.

1.2.21. 008 . . . .
100 1 ≠a Aarons, Lettie.
245 10 ≠a Ballad of true love : ≠b love is blind, etc.
250 ≠a 2nd ed.
260 ≠a Chicago : ≠b Field Museum Press, ≠c 1997.
300 ≠a x, 179 p. ; ≠c 30 cm.
504 ≠a Includes bibliographical references (p. 167-177) and index.

1.2.22. 008 . . . .
100 1 ≠a DeKing, Elizabeth.
245 10 ≠a Cry for me, my darlings.
260 ≠a London : ≠b Chidi Press, ≠c 1997.
300 ≠a 385 p., [36] p. of plates : ≠b col. ill. ; ≠c 30 cm.
504 ≠a Includes bibliographical references and index.

1.2.23. 008 . . . .
100 1 ≠a Morrison, Sylvia J.
245 10 ≠a Rage for age : ≠b the increasing elder generation.
250 ≠a 1st ed.
260 ≠a Washington, D.C. : ≠b Dept. of Health, Education, and Welfare ; for sale by the U.S. G.P.O., ≠c 1997.
300 ≠a 65 p. ; ≠c 28 cm.

1.2.24. 008 . . . .
100 1 ≠a Van Heusen, Phillips.
245 10 ≠a Beer for all! : ≠b and other campaign promises not kept.
260 ≠a Kansas City, MO : ≠b Beer Industry Press, ≠c 1996.
300 ≠a x, 309 p. : ≠b ill. ; ≠c 28 cm.
500 ≠a Includes index.

1.2.25. 008 . . . .

100	1	≠a Wilder, Genevieve.
245	10	≠a Mothers know best.
260		≠a Good Living, AK : ≠b Snow Press, ≠c 1997.
300		≠a 125 p., [48] p. of plates : ≠b col. ill. ; ≠c 28 cm.

1.3. Indicators

100 _	Personal name	110 _	Corporate name	111 _	Conference
0	Single forename	1	Place name	2	Direct
1	Surname	2	Direct order		

245 _ 1st indicator: Title tracing 1 = Yes, 0 = No *[title main entry is coded 0]*
_ 2nd indicator: Number of spaces to skip in indexing

250 Indicators are blank

260 Indicators are blank

300 Indicators are blank

440 _ Series title traced, 2nd indicator, number of spaces skipped

490 _ Series title not traced, or traced differently
1st indicator: 0 = not traced, 1 = traced differently *[if coded 1, 8xx must be present]*

500 Indicators are blank

504 Indicators are blank

505 _ 1st indicator: 0 = entire contents, 1 = partial contents

520 Indicators are blank

6xx Second indicator: 0 = LCSH, 1 = Annotated cards, 8 = Sears

600 Same 1st indicators as 100 field

610 Same 1st indicators as 110 field

611 Same 1st indicators as 111 field

650 No 1st indicator

651 No 1st indicator

7xx

700, 710, 711 1st indicator same as 1xx; 2nd indicator blank

740 1st indicator: number of spaces to skip; *[coded zero—no initial articles used]*
2nd indicator: 2 *[analytical entry]*

8xx Series traced differently

1.4. Tagging Exercises

Add the proper tags, indicators, and subfields to the data given below. The blanks indicate where tags, indicators, and subfields should be placed. Precede each subfield code with a delimiter. You will need to use the USMARC bibliographic formats, *AACR2r*, *LCSH*, or other tools. The first one in each section has been done for you.

Main entries

1.4.1. 100 1 ≠a Jones, Jessie.

1.4.2. 1___ _ ___ Garcia Lorca, Jose.

1.4.3. 1___ _ ___ Louisiana. ___ Legislature. ___ Senate.

1.4.4. 1___ _ ___ Louisiana Academy of Sciences.

1.4.5. 1___ _ ___ Kisatchie National Forest.

1.4.6. 1___ _ ___ Petrovsky, Alexandrovitch, ___ 1902-

1.4.7. 1___ _ ___ Spate, Gaspar J. ___ (Gaspar Julius), ___ 1881–1956.

1.4.8. 1___ _ ___ Paul, ___ of Byzantium.

1.4.9. 1___ _ ___ Balfa Brothers (Musical group)

1.4.10. 1___ _ ___ Shreveport (La.). ___ Police Jury. ___ Library Committee.

1.4.11. 1___ _ ___ Regional Planning Council for Southwest Louisiana.

1.4.12. 1___ _ ___ Nixon, Richard M.

1.4.13. 1___ _ ___ Pennyfeather, John, ___ Sir, ___1770-1820.

1.4.14. 1___ _ ___ Monroe Bowling Tournament ___ (1983 : ___ Monroe, La.)

Title statements

1.4.15. 245 1 0 ≠a Guide to writing tree ordinances / ≠c prepared by Buck Abbey.

1.4.16. 245 _ _ ___ “Blood will tell!” / ___ Joseph Bosco.

1.4.17. 245 _ _ ___ Reflections in time / ___ Elizabeth Crane, editor.

1.4.18. 245 _ _ ___ The vampire companion / ___ Katherine Ramsland.

1.4.19. 245 _ _ ___ The "Gimme something mister" guide to Mardi Gras / ___ by Arthur Hardy.

1.4.20. 245 _ _ ___ Guide de Nouvelle Orleans ___ [sound recording] = ___ Guide to New Orleans / ___ by John Candy.

1.4.21. 245 _ _ ___ Tell me more ; or, The Hollywood gossip book / ___ by Nancy Davis Reagan.

1.4.22. 245 _ _ ___ The stumpin' grounds : ___ a memoir of New Orleans' Ninth Ward / ___ by Russell E. Wyman.

1.4.23. 245 _ _ ___ ... So I told him no : ___ the trail to the Vice-Presidency / ___ by Al Gore.

1.4.24. 245 _ _ ___ Fort Claiborne / ___ prepared by Cecil Atkinson.

1.4.25. 245 _ _ ___ Hobnails and helmets / ___ William H. Burkhart ... [et al.].

1.4.26. 245 _ _ ___ The analysis of the law / ___ Sir Matthew Hale.

1.4.27. 245 _ _ ___ BBC adult literacy handbook / ___ edited by Chris Longley.

Publication, Distribution, etc.

1.4.28. 260 ≠a New York : ≠b Greenwillow Press, ≠c [1949].

1.4.29. 260 ___ Washington D.C. : ___ U.S. Department of Agriculture : [for sale by the U.S. G.P.O.], ___ 1964.

1.4.30. 260 ___ London : ___ Haynes ; ___ Brookstone, Ct. : ___ Auto Museum, ___ c1997.

1.4.31. 260 ___ [Bohemia, La.?] : ___ L.B. Oppenheimer, ___ 1957.

1.4.32. 260 ___ [Baton Rouge] : ___ Louisiana State University Press, ___ 1985.

1.4.33. 260 ___ Toronto ; New York : ___ Bantam, ___ c1952.

1.4.34. 260 ___ [S.l. : ___ s.n.], ___ 1935.

1.4.35. 260 ___ Paris : ___ LeBlanc et cie., ___ 1935, c1899.

1.4.36. 260 ___ Bayou Manchac, La. : ___ [s.n., ___ 19--?]

1.4.37. 260 ___ Alexandria, La. : ___ Alexandria Museum of Art, ___ c1977.

Physical Description

1.4.38. 300 ≠a 3 v. ; ≠c 30 cm. + ≠e atlas (301 leaves of plates : maps)

1.4.39. 300 ___ 64 p. : ___ maps ; ___ 32 cm.

1.4.40. 300 ___ 65 leaves, 102 p., [8] p. of plates : ___ ill. ; ___ 16 cm.

1.4.41. 300 ___ xlv, 789 p. : ___ ill., ports., maps (1 fold.) ; ___ 13 cm.

1.4.42. 300 ___ 251 p. ; ___ 22 cm.

1.4.43. 300 ___ 1 videocassette (22 min.) : ___ sd., col. ; ___ 1/2 in.

1.4.44. 300 ___ 1 microscope slide : ___ glass ; ___ 8 x 3 cm.

1.4.45. 300 ___ 1 game (15 pieces) : ___ col., cardboard ; ___ 9 x 12 in.

1.4.46. 300 ___ v. : ___ ill., maps ; ___ 28 cm.

1.4.47. 300 ___ 2 film reels (60 min. ea.) : ___ sd., b&w ; ___ 16 mm.

1.4.48. 300 ___ ii, 14, vi, 61 p. : ___ ill., facsims. ; ___ 16 x 12 cm.

1.4.49. 300 ___ 1 score : ___ 16 p. of music ; ___ 28 cm.

1.4.50. 300 ___ 1 v. (various pagings) ; ___ 26 cm.

1.4.51. 300 ___ 1 sound disc (65 min.) : ___ digital, stereo. ; ___4 3/4 in.

Series statement

1.4.52. 440 _ 0 ≠a Preservation guide

1.4.53. 4___ _ _ ___ Fodor guidebook series

1.4.54. 4___ _ _ ___ Nicholls State University. ___ Center for Traditional Louisiana Boatbuilding. ___ Wooden boat series

1.4.55. 4___ _ _ ___ Report / University of Southwestern Louisiana. Center for Archaeological Studies

1.4.56. 4__ _ _ ___ Water resources series. ___ North Louisiana subseries.

1.4.57. 4__ _ _ ___ Research / Louisiana State Dept. of Education. Vocational Education Section.

1.4.58. 4__ _ _ ___ State practice series

Notes

1.4.59. 5*00* *≠a* Title from disk label.

1.4.60. 5__ ___ Summary: Biography of Shaquille O'Neal.

1.4.61. 5__ ___ With: Only in your arms / Lisa Kleypas.

1.4.62. 5__ ___ Includes discography (p. 547-569).

1.4.63. 5__ ___ Title supplied by cataloger.

1.4.64. 5__ ___ Reprint. Originally published: Boston : Grey, 1896.

1.4.65. 5__ ___ Cast: Ronald Reagan, Bill Clinton, Richard Nixon.

1.4.66. 5__ _ ___ Contents: Hey look me over -- Louisiana hayride -- Cajun two-step -- When the saints go marching in -- Bayou blues -- LSU alma mater.

1.4.67. 5__ ___ Ph.D. (Library Science)--Duke University, 1978.

1.4.68. 5__ ___ Includes index.

1.4.69. 5__ ___ Editor, 1987- : Bobby Ferguson.

Subject Descriptors

1.4.70. 6*00* *1* *0* *≠a* Nixon, Richard M.

1.4.71. 6__ _ _ ___ Gardening ___ Louisiana ___ New Orleans.

1.4.72. 6__ _ _ ___ Louisiana. ___ Office of the Lieutenant Governor.

1.4.73. 6__ _ _ ___ State Library of Louisiana. ___ Technical Services Branch.

1.4.74. 6__ _ _ ___ Cookery (Oysters)

1.4.75. 6___ _ _ ___ Daughters of the Confederacy. ___ Louisiana Chapter. ___ Baton Rouge Post.

1.4.76. 6___ _ _ ___ Port Allen (La.) ___ Politics and government.

1.4.77. 6___ _ _ ___ Alexandria (La.) ___ History ___ Civil War, 1861-1865.

1.4.78. 6___ _ _ ___ Lawrence, Elizabeth, ___ 1904-1985.

1.4.79. 6___ _ _ ___ Physically handicapped artists ___ Louisiana.

1.4.80. 6___ _ _ ___ Ferguson family.

1.4.81. 6___ _ _ ___ Paul M. Hebert Law Center.

1.4.82. 6___ _ _ ___ Lafourche Parish (La.) __ Description and travel.

1.4.83. 6___ _ _ ___ Lafayette Parish (La.). ___ Office of the Mayor.

1.4.84. 6___ _ _ ___ New Tickfaw Baptist Church (Livingston Parish, La.)

1.4.85. 6___ _ _ ___ Joan, ___ of Arc, Saint.

1.4.86. 6___ _ _ ___ Pilottown (La.) ___ History.

1.4.87. 6___ _ _ ___ Hunter, Bruce, ___1958-

1.4.88. 6___ _ _ ___ East Feliciana Parish (La.) ___ Economic aspects.

1.4.89. 6___ _ _ ___ Hurricanes ___ Louisiana ___ Cheniere Caminada.

1.4.90. 6___ _ _ ___ Grand Isle Tarpon Rodeo ___ (26th : ___ 1979)

1.4.91. 6___ _ _ ___ Bible. ___ O.T. ___ Genesis.

Full records

The records below are full bibliographic records. Although there are lines for you to use in identifying fields, indicators, and subfields, there are no examples. Use the preceding exercises to help fill in the full records.

1.4.92.

110 _ _ ___ Alabama. ___ Alcoholic Beverage Control Board.

245 _ _ ___ Annual beer report / ___ Alabama Alcoholic Beverage Control Board.

260 ___ Montgomery, Ala. : ___ The Board.

300 ___ v. ; ___ 28 cm.

310 ___ Annual.

500 ___ Description based on: October 1, 1977-Sept. 30, 1978.

500 ___ Title from cover.

500 ___ Report year ends Sept. 30.

650 _ _ ___ Brewing industry ___ Alabama ___ Statistics.

1.4.93.

245 _ _ ___ Marching bands & corps.

246 _ _ ___ Marching bands and corps.

260 ___ [Jacksonville, Fla. : ___ River City Publications], ___ 1967-

300 ___ v. : ___ ill. ; ___ 28 cm.

310 ___ Monthly.

362 _ ___ 1967-

500 ___ Includes index.

650 _ _ ___ Bands (Music)

1.4.94.

100 _ ___ Milne, A. A. ___ (Alan Alexander), ___ 1882–1956.

245 _ _ ___ The house at Pooh Corner / ___ by A.A. Milne ; illustrated by Kate Greenaway.

260 ___ Chicago, Ill. : ___ Childrens Press, ___ c1983.

300 ___ 128 p. : ___ ill. ; ___ 21 cm.

440 _ _ ___ World's greatest classics

700 _s ___ Greenaway, Kate.

1.4.95.

100 _ ___ Grahame, Kenneth.

245 _ _ ___ The wind in the willows / ___ by Kenneth Grahame ; illustrated by Robert J. Lee.

260 ___ New York : ___ Dell, ___ 1973, c1969.

300 ___ 244 p. : ___ ill. ; ___ 19 cm.

500 ___ "A Yearling book."

The next group of bibliographic records has only the first digit of the tag. You are to supply the complete tag, the indicators, and the subfields. Lines are given for your assistance in placing subfield tags.

1.4.96.

1__ _ ___ Alford, Gilbert K.

2__ _ _ ___ Alford ancestors and descendants : ___ Jacob and Alvina Alford, the Allfords, and related families / ___ by Gil and Anna Alford.

2__ ___ Rev. ed., with corrections.

2__ ___ [S.l.] : ___ G.K. Alford, ___ [1986?]

3__ ___ x, 279 p. : ___ ports., facsims., geneal. tables ; ___ 28 cm.

5__ ___ Includes indexes.

6__ _ _ ___ Alford family.

6__ _ _ ___ Red River Parish (La.) ___ Genealogy.

6__ _ _ ___ Marriage records ___ Louisiana ___ Red River Parish.

7__ _ _ ___ Alford, Anna.

1.4.97.

1__ _ ___ Stratton, Joanna L.

2__ _ _ ___ Pioneer women : ___ voices from the Kansas frontier / ___ Joanna L. Stratton ; introduced by Arthur M. Schlesinger, Jr.

2__ ___ 1st ed.

2__ ___ New York : ___ Simon & Schuster, ___ c1981.

3__ ___ 319 p., [16] leaves of plates : ___ ill. ; ___ 24 cm.

5__ ___ Includes bibliographical references (p. [305]-307) and index.

6__ _ _ ___ Women ___ Kansas ___ History.

6__ _ _ ___ Pioneers ___ Kansas ___ History.

1.4.98.

2__ _ _ ___ The Bishop's bounty / ___ compiled by The Bishop's Bounty Cookbook Committee, Saint Mary's Parents' Group, Inc., Saint Mary's Training School for Retarded Children.

2__ ___ Alexandria, La. : ___ Saint Mary's Parents' Group, ___ c1987.

3__ ___ 318 p. : ___ ill. ; ___ 24 cm.

5__ ___ Includes index.

6__ _ _ ___ Cookery, American ___ Louisiana style.

7__ _ _ ___ Saint Mary's Training School for Retarded Children (Alexandria, La.). ___ Saint Mary's Parents' Group.

1.4.99.

2___ _ _ ___ Les blues de Balfa ___ [videorecording] : ___ with Cajun visits/ Visites Cajun.

2__ ___ San Francisco, Calif. : __ Aginsky Productions, ___ c1983, c1981.

3__ ___ 1 videocassette (20, 16 min.) : ___ sd., col. ; ___ 1/2 in.

5__ ___ VHS format.

5__ ___ Summary: The story of the Balfa Brothers, and a visit to Cajun country.

6___ _ _ ___ Cajuns ___ Louisiana.

6___ _ _ ___ Balfa, Dewey.

6___ _ _ ___ Balfa Brothers (Musical group)

7___ _ _ ___ Cajun visits.

7___ _ _ ___ Visites Cajun.

The last two bibliographic records have no tags, no indicators, no subfields, and no lines to help you place the subfield delimiters in the correct places. Use the preceding examples, and you're on your own. Good luck!

1.4.100.

___ _ Darensbourg, Joe, 1906-1985.

___ _ _ Jazz odyssey : the autobiography of Joe Darensbourg / as told to Peter Vacher.

___ _ _ Telling it like it is.

___ Baton Rouge : Louisiana State University Press, 1988, c1987.

___ vi, 231 p., [32] p. of plates : ports. ; 25 cm.

___ Includes bibliographical references (p. [197]-207) and index.

___ Published in England under the title: Telling it like it is.

___ _ _ Darensbourg, Joe, 1906-1985.

___ _ _ Jazz musicians Louisiana New Orleans.

___ _ _ Vacher, Peter, 1937-

1.4.101.

___ _ Kilbourne, Richard Holcomb.

___ _ _ A history of the Louisiana Civil Code : the formative years, 1803-1839 / Richard Holcomb Kilbourne, Jr.

___ [Baton Rouge] : Publications Institute, Paul M. Hebert Law Center, Louisiana State University, c1987.

___ xv, 268 p. ; 24 cm.

___ "Prepared under the auspices of the Center of Civil Law Studies."--t.p.

___ Includes bibliographical references and index.

___ _ _ Civil law Louisiana History.

___ _ _ Civil law Louisiana Codification History.

___ _ _ Paul M. Hebert Law Center.

1.5. Series

A series is a group of separate bibliographic items which are related to each other in some manner and which may or may not be numbered. It may be a group of articles, memoirs, essays, or other writings issued in sequence, or a separately numbered sequence of volumes. A series may be by a single author or by many authors. The name of a series may indicate the subject matter or the publisher that the items have in common, or it may be a generic designation such as Report, Bulletin, or Proceedings. The authorized form of the series name may be different from the way it is printed on the item being cataloged. Using a series tracing gives searchers another access point in the bibliographic record.

There are five fields for series statements in the MARC format.

400 Series entry, personal name

410 Series entry, corporate name

411 Series entry, meeting name

440 Series entry, title

490 Series statement traced differently or not traced at all

When a 490 series statement is used, the first indicator position tells whether the series is not traced (0) or is traced differently (1). When a series is traced differently, an 8xx field MUST be present in the record.

Coding for the different types of series statements is given below, followed by exercises to reinforce your knowledge of the codes.

400 Series Statement/Added Entry—Personal Name

Indicators

First: Type of personal name entry element
0—Forename
1—Surname
3—Family surname

Second: Pronoun represents main entry. A value that indicates whether a possessive pronoun is used to represent the author of the series
0—Main entry not represented by pronoun
1—Main entry represented by pronoun. The author portion of the series statement contains a possessive pronoun that refers to the name in the 1xx field. The first indicator value is based on the type of name entry element in the 1xx field.

Subfield Codes

a—Personal name

b—Numeration

c—Titles and other words associated with a name

d—Dates associated with a name

e—Relator term

f—Date of a work

g—Miscellaneous information

k—Form subheading

l—Language of a work

n—Number of part/section of a work

p—Name of part/section of a work

t—Title of a work

u—Affiliation

v—Volume number/sequential designation

x—International Standard Serial Number

4—Relator code

6—Linkage

Examples

400 10 ≠a Wines, David G., ≠d 1940- . ≠t Ideas for self-employment
400 10 ≠a Shakespeare, William, ≠d 1564-1616. ≠t Poems
400 11 ≠a Her ≠t Travels in many lands ; ≠v vol. 16
400 11 ≠a His ≠t Letters from Kathmandu

410 Series Statement/Added Entry—Corporate Name

Indicators

First: Type of corporate name entry element
1—Jurisdiction name
2—Name in direct order

Second: Pronoun represents main entry
0—Main entry not represented by pronoun
1—Main entry represented by pronoun

Subfield Codes

a—Corporate name or jurisdiction name as entry element
b—Subordinate unit
c—Location of meeting
d—Date of meeting or treaty signing
e—Relator term
f—Date of a work
g—Miscellaneous information
k—Form subheading
l—Language of a work
n—Number of part/section/meeting
p—Name of part/section/meeting
t—Title of work
u—Affiliation
v—Volume number/sequential designation
x—International Standard Serial number
4—Relator code
6—Linkage

Examples

410 10 ≠a Jefferson (Tex.). ≠b Office of the Mayor. ≠t Historic buildings and their contents ; ≠v v. 7
410 11 ≠a Its ≠t Research bulletin, ≠v 78-RB-3
410 21 ≠a Its ≠t Report ; ≠v no. 1 ≠x 0141-9676

411 Series Statement/Added Entry—Meeting Name

Indicators

First: Type of meeting name entry element
0—Inverted name
1—Jurisdiction name
2—Name in direct order

Second: Pronoun represents main entry
0—Main entry not represented by pronoun
1—Main entry represented by pronoun

Subfield Codes

a—Meeting name or jurisdiction name as entry element
c—Location of meeting
d—Date of meeting
e—Subordinate unit
f—Date of a work
g—Miscellaneous information
k—Form subheading
l—Language of a work
n—Number of part/section/meeting
p—Name of part/section/meeting
q—Name of meeting following jurisdiction name entry element
t—Title of work
u—Affiliation
v—Volume number/sequential designation
x—International Standard Serial number
4—Relator code
6—Linkage

Examples

411 10 ≠a Chicago. ≠q Cartography Conference, ≠d 1974. ≠t Map ; ≠v no. 10 ≠x 0000-0000
411 10 ≠a International Labor Conference. ≠t Bulletin
411 21 ≠a Its ≠t Proceedings ; ≠v v. 2

440 Series Statement/Added Entry—Title

Indicators

First: Undefined
Contains a blank (_)
Second: Nonfiling characters
0–9—Number of nonfiling characters present

Subfield Codes

a—Title
n—Number of part/section of a work
p—Name of part/section of a work
v—Volume number/sequential designation
x—International Standard Serial number
6—Linkage

Examples

440 _0 ≠a Collection africaine
440 _0 ≠a Okonomische Studien ; ≠v Bd. 22
440 _4 ≠a The Pediatric clinics of North America ; ≠v v. 2, no. 4

440 _0 ≠a Journal of polymer science. ≠n Part C, ≠p Polymer symposia ; ≠v no. 39
440 _4 ≠a The Rare book tapes. ≠n Series 1 ; ≠v 5
440 _0 ≠a Janua linguarum. ≠p Series major, ≠x 0075-3114 ; ≠v 100
440 _0 ≠a Romanica Gothoburgensia, ≠x 0080-3683 ; ≠v 12, 16

490 Series Statement/Traced Differently or Not at All

Indicators

First: Specifies whether series is traced
0—Series not traced
1—Series traced differently. Record contains a corresponding 800–830 series added entry field

Second: Undefined; contains a blank (_)

Subfield Codes

a—Series statement; a series title that may also contain a statement of responsibility, other title information, dates, or volume numbers preceding or appearing as part of the title
l—Library of Congress call number; an LC series call number that is used for a serial that has been issued as part of the series
v—Volume number/sequential designation
x—International Standard Serial number
6—Linkage

Examples

490 0_ ≠a Pelican books
490 0_ ≠a Computer indexed marriage records
490 1_ ≠a Uniform crime reports
490 1_ ≠a Department of the Army pamphlet ; ≠v 27-50
490 1_ ≠a [1981-]: Reference works
490 1_ ≠a Bulletin / U.S. Department of Labor, Bureau of Labor Statistics
490 1_ ≠a Annual census of manufactures = ≠a Recensement des manufactures. ≠x 0315-5587
490 1_ ≠a Map / Geological Survey of Alabama ; ≠v 158, plate 3
490 1_ ≠a West Virginia University bulletin ; ≠v ser. 74, no. 11-3. ≠t Bulletin / Experiment Station, West Virginia University ; ≠v 111

800 Series Added Entry—Personal Name

Indicators

First: Type of personal name entry element
0—Forename
1—Surname
3—Family surname

Second: Undefined
Contains a blank (_)

Subfield Codes

a—Personal name
b—Numeration
c—Titles and other words associated with a name
d—Dates associated with a name
e—Relator term
f—Date of a work
g—Miscellaneous information
h—Medium *[general material designator for media]*
k—Form subheading
l—Language of a work
m—Medium of performance for music
n—Number of part/section of a work
o—Arranged statement for music
p—Name of part/section of a work
q—Fuller form of name
r—Key for music
s—Version
t—Title of a work
u—Affiliation
v—Volume number/sequential designation
4—Relator code
6—Linkage

Examples

800 1_ ≠a Berenholtz, Jim, ≠d 1957- . ≠t Teachings of the feathered serpent ; ≠v bk. 1
800 1_ ≠a Poe, Edgar Allan, ≠d 1809-1849. ≠t Works. ≠l German. ≠f 1922. ≠s Rosl ; ≠v 1. Bd.
800 1_ ≠a Joyce, James, ≠d 1882-1941. ≠t James Joyce archive
800 1_ ≠a Darnell, Jack. ≠t Edible wild plants of the planet earth
800 1_ ≠a Armstrong, Louis, ≠d 1900-1971. ≠4 prf. ≠t Louie Armstrong (Universal City Studios) ; ≠v 6

810 Series Added Entry—Corporate Name

Indicators

First: Type of corporate name entry element
1—Jurisdiction name
2—Name in direct order

Second: Undefined
Contains a blank (_)

Subfield Codes

a—Corporate name or jurisdiction name as entry element
b—Subordinate unit

c—Location of meeting
d—Date of meeting or treaty signing
e—Relator term
f—Date of a work
g—Miscellaneous information
h—Medium
k—Form subheading
l—Language of a work
m—Medium of performance for music
n—Number of part/section/meeting
o—Arranged statement for music
p—Name of part/section/meeting
r—Key for music
s—Version
t—Title of work
u—Affiliation
v—Volume number/sequential designation
4—Relator code
6—Linkage

Examples

810 2_ ≠a John Bartholomew and Son. ≠t Bartholomew world travel series ; ≠v 10
810 2_ ≠a Central Institute of Indian Languages. ≠t CIIL linguistic atlas series ; ≠v 1
810 2_ ≠a European Court of Human Rights. ≠t Publications de la Cour europeenne des droits de l'homme. ≠n Serie A, ≠p Arrets et decisions ; ≠v vol. 48
810 1_ ≠a United States. ≠b Army Map Service. ≠t A.M.S. ; ≠v Z201

811 Series Added Entry—Meeting Name

Indicators

First: Type of meeting name entry element
1—Jurisdiction name
2—Name in direct order

Second: Undefined
Contains a blank (_)

Subfield Codes

a—Meeting name or jurisdiction name as entry element
c—Location of meeting
d—Date of meeting
e—Subordinate unit
f—Date of a work
g—Miscellaneous information
h—Medium
k—Form subheading

l—Language of a work
n—Number of part/section/meeting
p—Name of part/section/meeting
q—Name of meeting following jurisdiction name entry element
s—Version
t—Title of work
u—Affiliation
v—Volume number/sequential designation
4—Relator code
6—Linkage

Examples

811 2_ ≠a International Congress of Romance Linguistics and Philology ≠n (17th : ≠d 1983 : ≠e Aix-en-Provence, France). ≠t Actes du XVIISme Congress International de linguistique et philologie romanes ; ≠v vol. no. 5

811 2_ ≠a International Congress of Nutrition ≠n (11th : ≠d 1978 : ≠c Rio de Janeiro, Brazil). ≠t Nutrition and food science ; ≠v v. 1

811 2_ ≠a Delaware Symposium on Language Studies. ≠t Delaware symposia on language studies ; ≠v 4

830 Series Added Entry—Uniform Title

Indicators

First: Undefined
Contains a blank (_)

Second: Nonfiling characters
0–9—Number of nonfiling characters present

Subfield Codes

a—Uniform title
d—Date of treaty signing
f—Date of a work
g—Miscellaneous information
h—Medium
k—Form subheading
l—Language of a work
m—Medium of performance for music
n—Number of part/section of a work
o—Arranged statement for music
p—Name of part/section of a work
r—Key for music
s—Version
t—Title of a work *[a title-page title of a work]*
v—Volume number/sequential designation
6—Linkage

Examples

830 _0 ≠a Resources information series
830 _0 ≠a Imago (Series)
830 _0 ≠a Sport (International Union of Students. Physical Education and Sports Dept.) ; ≠v v. 10
830 _0 ≠a Monograph (University of California, Los Angeles. Dept. of Continuing Education in Health Sciences)
830 _0 ≠a Musica de camera (Oxford University Press) ; ≠v 72
830 _0 ≠a Basic nursing skills (Robert J. Brady Company) ; ≠v tape 14
830 _0 ≠a Teenage years ≠h [videorecording]

Series Exercises

Take the following series entries and reformat them for each tag given. Watch the indicators and construct the entries accordingly.

1.5.1. 440 _0 ≠a Rechtschistorisch Instituut (Series). ≠n Serie 1

490 0_ ______________________________

1.5.2. 410 20 ≠a State University of New York. ≠t SUNY series in new directions in crime and justice studies.

440 _0 ______________________________

1.5.3. 490 1_ ≠a Defense of usury / Jeremy Bentham, 1748-1832.

800 1_ ______________________________

440 _0 ______________________________

1.5.4. 490 1_ ≠a AAR studies in religion (American Academy of Religion)

440 _0 ______________________________

490 1_ ______________________________

810 2_ ______________________________

1.5.5. 400 10 ≠a Moyes, Patricia. ≠t Inspector Henry Tibbett mystery

440 _0 ______________________________

In the next group of exercises you are given author and/or series title information. Use the information to create the series entry in the tag you are given. Use correct subfield delimiters.

1.5.6. Author: Lane, Roger.
Series title: History of crime and criminal justice series

400 10 ______________________________

1.5.7. Author: Horne, Diane.
Series title: Prehistoric animals, volume 3

440 _0 ______________________________

1.5.8. Author: Probity, Suellen.
Series title: Medical problems
Sub-series title: Part 2, Blood problems

490 1_ ______________________________

____

800 1_ ______________________________

____

1.5.9. Author: Smith, J. Wesley.
Series title: Contemporary questions

490 0_ ______________________________

1.5.10. Author: Lambert, Stephen E.
Series title: VGM career books
Publisher: VGM Career Horizons

490 1_ ______________________________

830 1_ ______________________________

1.5.11. Author: Watters, Thomas R.
Series title: Smithsonian guides

440 _0 ______________________________

1.5.12. Author: Muddy, Juan Bigge.
Series title: A Macmillan reference book

490 1_ ________________________________

830 _0 ________________________________

1.5.13. Author: Conover, Ernie.
Series title on cover: Woodworking plans series
Series title on title page: Betterway woodworking plans series

490 0_ ________________________________

490 1_ ________________________________

830 _0 ________________________________

1.5.14. Author: Wiencek, Henry.
Series title from title page: Volume one of The Smithsonian guide to historic America

440 _4 ________________________________

1.5.15. Author: Steinberg, Eve P.
Series title: Civil service test tutor, Arco Publishing House

490 1_ ________________________________

830 _0 ________________________________

1.5.16. Author: Freeman, Kerry A.
Series title: Chilton Book Company, Chilton's total car care

440 _0 ________________________________

490 0_ ________________________________

1.5.17. Author: Mitchell Manuals, inc.
Series title: Mitchell manuals for the automotive professional

440 _0 ________________________________

1.5.18. Author: Zapata, Hector.
Series title from cover: Louisiana State University Agricultural Center, Louisiana Agricultural Experiment Station, Dept. of Agricultural Economics and Agribusiness, Research Report.
Series title from title page: D.A.E. research report

440 _0 ____________________

490 0_ ____________________

1.5.19. Author: Henning, Steven Alan.
Series title from cover: Department of Agricultural Economics and Agribusiness, Louisiana State University Agricultural Center, Louisiana Agricultural Experiment Station, information series
Series title from title page: A.E.A. information series

490 1_ ____________________

830 _0 ____________________

1.5.20. Author: Sewell, Willie.
Series title: Guitar tunes for country players

490 1_ ____________________

800 1_ ____________________

1.6. Error Identification Exercises

There is one error on each line. The errors will be in the tag, the indicators, or the subfields. Circle the error, then write the correction on the line.

1.6.1. 100 1 ≠a Smith, John, ≠z 1956- ________

1.6.2. 110 2 ≠a Garcia Williams, John. ________

1.6.3. 110 2 ≠a Port Allen (La.). ≠b Parish Council. ________

1.6.4. 100 2 ≠a Minnie Pearl, ≠d 1921-1967. ________

1.6.5. 111 1 ≠a Basketball championship ≠d (1995). ________

1.6.6. 240 12 ≠a A dictionary of dogs. ________

1.6.7. 245 10 ≠a The horse runs / ≠c John Equus. ________

1.6.8.	245 14	≠a Everybody wins! / ≠c Polly Tishan.	________
1.6.9.	246 14	≠a You @#$%^&*!!!	________
1.6.10.	245 12	≠a A man for all seasons / ≠b Jim Doe.	________
1.6.11.	260	≠a New York : ≠b c1996.	________
1.6.12.	260	≠a Libraries Unlimited, ≠c c1996.	________
1.6.13.	260	≠a Converse, La. : ≠b Lewis Pub., ≠d c1990.	________
1.6.14.	260 0	≠a Gem, KS : ≠b J.W. Pub. Co., ≠c c1982.	________
1.6.15.	300	≠a 123 p. : ≠c ill. ; ≠c 22 cm	________
1.6.16.	300	≠a 54 p. ; ≠b 25 cm.	________
1.6.17.	300	≠b 2 v. ; ≠c 26 cm.	________
1.6.18.	300	≠a 145 p. : ≠b maps, ill. ; ≠c 1965-	________
1.6.19.	301	≠a 13 v. : ≠b ill. ; ≠c 25 cm.	________
1.6.20.	600 20	≠a Ferguson, A. S. ≠q (Anna S.)	________
1.6.21.	650 10	≠a Basketball ≠x History.	________
1.6.22.	650 0	≠a Indiana ≠x Description and travel.	________
1.6.23.	610 20	≠a Art for New Artists Conference.	________
1.6.24.	651 0	≠x Alaska ≠x Politics and government.	________
1.6.25.	650 0	≠a Automobiles ≠y Maintenance and repair.	________
1.6.26.	651 20	≠a Bible ≠x Commentaries.	________
1.6.27.	611 20	≠a International Film Festival ≠p (1996)	________
1.6.28.	600 20	≠a Annette (Actress)	________
1.6.29.	653 0	≠a Detective and mystery stories.	________
1.6.30.	650 0	≠y Twentieth century.	________
1.6.31.	651 20	≠a Chicago Bulls.	________
1.6.32.	630 00	≠t Bible. ≠p O.T. ≠p Psalms ≠x Commentaries	________

Multiple Errors Exercises

Find all the errors on each line. Circle them, then write the correct form above the error.

1.6.33.	100 1	≠a Smith-Rosen, G. N. ≠p (Guy Ngo)
1.6.34.	110 2	≠a Many (La.). ≠c Mayor.
1.6.35.	100 1	≠q Smith, John Bob, ≠y 1901-1946.
1.6.36.	111 1	≠a Golf days ≠n (10th : ≠d 1990 ; ≠c Many (La.)
1.6.37.	110 2	≠a Louisiana. ≠a Office of Marine Fisheries.
1.6.38.	245 00	≠a The tale of two kitties / ≠c by Mama Cat.
1.6.39.	245 00	≠b Dogs : ≠b a long tale / ≠c compiled by John Reeder.
1.6.40.	240 10	≠a The sound and the fury / ≠b Ralph Nader.
1.6.41.	245 15	≠a Les miserables / ≠c illustrated by Pablo Picasso.
1.6.42.	246 14	≠a The soccer defeat : ≠b by the Boston Jets.
1.6.43.	260 0	≠a New York : ≠b Milwaukee, ≠b c1946, ≠c 1982.
1.6.44.	261	≠a Many ; ≠a Shreveport ; ≠a Reeves, ≠a c1996.
1.6.45.	260	New York : ≠b Viking, ≠b 1693.
1.6.46.	260	≠a Viking Press : ≠b New York ; ≠c 28 cm.
1.6.47.	260	≠x Baton Rouge : ≠a Ferguson Frolics, ≠y c1992.
1.6.48.	300 1	≠a 2 v. ; ≠a ill., maps, ports ; ≠b 8 in.
1.6.49.	301	≠a x, 145, vi, 632, ix, 15 p. ; ≠b 22 cm.
1.6.50.	300	≠a 92 p. : ≠b col. ill., facsims. ; ≠z 28 x 22 cm.
1.6.51.	300	≠a : ≠b
1.6.52.	300	≠a [S.l.] : ≠b [s.n.], ≠c [1995].
1.6.53.	600 10	≠a Smith, J. B. ≠x (John Bob), ≠y 1952-
1.6.54.	610 10	≠a Louisiana Rodeo Association.
1.6.55.	611 10	≠a Lutcher Rodeo Days (≠a 1st : ≠d 1996 ; ≠b Lutcher, La.)

1.6.56. 650 0 ≠a Sabine Parish (La.)

1.6.57. 651 0 ≠a Louisiana ≠z Description.

1.6.58. 650 0 ≠a Cherokee Indians ≠y History, 18th century.

1.6.59. 600 00 ≠a Jeremiah ≠x (Fictitious character) ≠x Fiction.

1.6.60. 600 00 ≠a F'lar, ≠q of Pern, ≠c Dragonrider.

1.6.61. 651 0 ≠a Louisiana ≠b Office of Tourism.

1.6.62. 600 10 ≠a Jones family ≠x Genealogy.

1.6.63. 600 20 ≠a Smith, Robbie, ≠x Biography.

1.6.64. 610 20 ≠a Baton Rouge, Lousiana : ≠b Mayor.

1.6.65. 630 00 ≠t Bible, N.T., Matthew.

The number of errors in each record is given in parentheses at the top of the record. Find the errors and circle them. The errors may be in spelling, tags, indicators, subfields, punctuation, etc.

1.6.66. (10)

100 1 ≠a Smith, James D., ≠c 1956-

245 14 ≠a Dogs of the world / ≠c by Jim Smith, Jr.

250 ≠a First edition.

260 ≠a N.Y. : ≠bViking Press, ≠c1995.

300 ≠a ix, 256 p. ; ≠c col. ill., ≠c c1995.

440 0 ≠t Animals of the world.

500 ≠a Includes index.

650 0 ≠a Dogs ≠z Encyclopedias.

1.6.67. (11)

110 2 ≠a Louisiana. ≠p State Records Office.

240 10 ≠a Registry of state lands : ≠c Louisiana State Records Office.

250 ≠a 1996 ed.

260 ≠a Baton Rouge : ≠c The Office, ≠b 1996.

300 ≠a 1 v. (various pagings) ; ≠b 28 cm.

500 ≠a Cover title.

504 ≠c Includes index.

651 0 ≠a Louisiana ≠x Registers.

650 0 ≠a Land use ≠x Louisiana.

710 2 ≠a Louisiana. ≠b State Records Office.

1.6.68. (16)

110 1 ≠c Robb, Randall R.

245 04 ≠a The archer looses an arrow : ≠c by Randall R. Robb and Sturgis S. Stubbs.

246 30 ≠a Into the air.

250 ≠1st ed.

300 ≠a 540 p. ; ≠c 18 cm.

440 0 ≠t Soldiery

650 0 ≠a Detective and mystery stories.

651 0 ≠b Medieval fiction.

700 2 ≠a Stubbs, Sturgis S.

1.6.69. (19)

110 2 ≠a Wisconsin Library of the Arts.

245 14 ≠t Inventory control at the Library of the Arts : ≠c a manual of procedures / ≠b by the staff of the Wisconsin Library of the Arts.

300 00 ≠a 25 l. : ≠b ill. ; ≠b 11.5 in.

500 00 ≠a Includes index and bibliography.

650 00 ≠a Wisconsin. ≠b Library of the Arts ≠x Handbooks, manuals, etc.

650 00 ≠a Art. ≠x Preservation.

650 10 ≠x Books ≠x Repair.

710 2 ≠a Wisconsin Library of the Arts.

1.6.70. (7)

100 2 ≠a Michigan ≠b Dept. of Highways.

245 10 ≠a Michigan highways.

300 ≠v v. : ≠b ill., maps ; ≠c 28 cm.

321 ≠a Annual

362 0 ≠a Vol. 1, no. 1- (September 1852)-

500 ≠q Title from cover.

650 0 ≠x Michigan ≠x Periodicals.

1.6.71. (11)

110 2 _ ≠x Philadelphia (Pa.). ≠p City Council.

246 10 ≠a The early history of Philadelphia : ≠b from its founding to 1900.

250 ≠a * ed.

300 ≠a xix, 312 p., 16 pages of plates : ≠b ill., maps, ports. ; ≠c 28 cm.

650 _ 0 ≠b Philadelphia, Pennsylvania ≠x History and description.

1.6.72. (15)

245 10 ≠q Milne, A. G. ≠q Albert George.

245 10 ≠a The plane in Spane mainly falls ; ≠c A.G. Milne.

251 ≠a 16th edition

260 ≠a Little House Press, ≠d c1992.

300 ≠a xxxviii, 24 pages : ≠c ill., maps ; ≠c c1992.

651 1 ≠a Aircraft ≠x Spain.

1.6.73. (16)

110 _ 0 ≠a Gargantua, Draconus.

240 ≠a My life as the Black Dragon / ≠b Draconus Gargantua.

250 ≠a Munich, Germany : ≠b c1994.

300 ≠A 365 p. ; ≠b illus., gen. tables ; 27 cm.

490 _ 0 \a My life series.

650 0 _ ≠a Gargantua, Draconius.

1.6.74. (18)

100 10 ≠a Chan, Lois Mai.

244 14 ≠b Dewey decimal classfication / ≠b a practical guide / ◆c Lois Mai Chan ... [et. al.]

255 ≠a 2nd ed. Revised

266 ≠a Albany : ≠b Forest Press, ≠c 1996.

300 ≠A 322 p. ≠b 8 1/2 in.

500 ≠a Contains bibliographical references and index.

650 _ 0 ≠a Classification, Dewey decimal.

2.
ANGLO-AMERICAN CATALOGUING RULES

2nd edition, 1988 revision

Introduction

The *Anglo-American Cataloguing Rules*, second edition, commonly called *AACR2*, was published in 1978 and has been generally adopted by most English-speaking countries around the world. This acceptance is a result of the increasing use of networks and shared cataloging. The second edition has been translated, or is in the process of translation, into Arabic, Bahasa Malaysia, Chinese, Danish, Finnish, French, Italian, Japanese, Norwegian, Portuguese, Spanish, Swedish, Turkish, and Urdu. In 1988 a revision, usually called *AACR2R*, was published, and updates to the revision have been issued periodically. In early fall 1998, a new text incorporating these updates will be published. You should use the 1998 text with this workbook.

These cataloging rules were designed to cover the description and access points of all materials commonly collected at the present time. The first edition of *AACR* (published in 1967) was issued in two editions—a British text and a North American text. The second edition (1978) reconciled the British and North American texts as to style and spellings. Where Webster's *New International Dictionary*, the authority used for this edition, permitted an alternative British spelling (catalogue, centre), it has been used. Where the American usage is the only one specified, it has been used.

Part I deals with the provision of information describing the item being cataloged and Part II deals with the determination and establishment of headings (or access points) under which the descriptive information is to be presented to catalog users. The rules proceed from the general to the specific.

The basic rules for the description of all library materials are to be found in Chapter 1, followed by rules for specific types of material. The areas of description remain the same across chapters; for example, rule 1.5 contains information about the physical description of an item, rule 3.5 deals with physical description of cartographic materials, and rule 8.5 deals with physical description of graphic materials. This workbook uses the general rules in Chapter 1 and specific rules in Chapter 2, plus Part II, "Headings, Uniform Titles, and References." Chapters 3–10 of Part I are discussed in the *Cataloging Nonprint Materials* in the Blitz Cataloging Workbook Series.

Read rules 0.1–0.29 in *AACR2R*, then complete the following exercises.

2.1. *AACR2R* Areas Exercises

Use the Contents pages in *AACR2R* to answer the questions. Give the area number for each specified type of information. Use the format *x*.-- for your answer.

Example:
Facsimiles, photocopies, and other reproductions *x.11*

2.1.1. Title and statement of responsibility ________

2.1.2. Publication, distribution, etc. ________

2.1.3. Note area ________

2.1.4. Standard number and terms of availability area ________

2.1.5. General rules ________

2.1.6. Edition area ________

2.1.7. Supplementary items ________

2.1.8. Physical description area ________

2.1.9. Material (or type of publication) specific details area ________

2.1.10. Series area ________

2.1.11. Items made up of several types of material ________

2.1.12. Facsimiles, photocopies, and other reproductions ________

Write the title of each area, and the type of format each one represents.

Example:
4.4 *Manuscripts ; Publication, distribution, etc., area*

2.1.13. 1.2 ________________________________

2.1.14. 3.4 ________________________________

2.1.15. 9.1 ________________________________

2.1.16. 10.0 ________________________________

2.1.17. 6.3 ________________________________

2.1.18. 8.5 ______________________________

2.1.19. 2.6 ______________________________

2.1.20. 5.8 ______________________________

2.1.21. 4.7 ______________________________

2.1.22. 11.5 ______________________________

2.2. *AACR2R* General Exercises

Use the introductions to the various chapters in Parts I and II to answer the following questions.

2.2.1. Who was the editor of *Anglo-American Cataloguing Rules*, 2nd edition?

2.2.2. Who was the editor of the 1988 revision to *AACR2?*

2.2.3. Which rule covers the chief source of information? Use the format (x.--).

2.2.4. Which rule gives information on levels of detail in description? Use the format (x.--).

2.2.5. Which rule gives information on punctuation? Use the format (x.--).

2.2.6. How do I identify a transcription that contains an inaccuracy or a misspelled word?

2.2.7. Which rule tells me so?

2.2.8. Which rule tells me how to deal with multipart items? Use the format (x.--).

2.2.9. Which rule tells me how to organize the description of a work I am cataloging?

2.2.10. Do all libraries need to use uniform titles? Which rule tells me this?

2.2.11. Do I transcribe uniform titles from a nonroman script in roman script or nonroman script? Which rule tells me this?

2.2.12. Which rule tells me about the use of initial articles in uniform titles?

2.2.13. Does *AACR2R* tell me about assigning subject headings?

2.2.14. Which rule gives the list of general material designations (GMDs)?

2.2.15. Are general material designations usually used with books?

2.2.16. What is the authority used for those matters of style not covered by the rules? Which rule tells me this?

2.2.17. Do all the examples in *AACR2R* follow all the rules?

2.2.18. Where would I go to find corrections, additions, or interpretations of the rules in *AACR2R*?

2.2.19. Does *AACR2R* apply to manual or automated library catalogs, or both? Why?

2.2.20. What does the word *predominantly* mean when used in *AACR2R*? Which rule gives me this definition?

2.2.21. Does Chapter 23 apply to both geographic entities and corporate bodies?

2.2.22. Do you always have to make additions to personal names, such as birth and death dates, fuller forms of the name, or distinguishing phrases?

2.2.23. Will every chapter have specific rules for everything? If not, what do I do?

2.2.24. Do access points always tell what their specific form is; for example, main or added entry?

2.2.25. Is there a rule telling when you can use a corporate body as main entry? If so, which one?

2.3. *AACR2R*, Part I Exercises

Use Chapter 2, "Books, Pamphlets, and Printed Sheets," to answer the following questions.

2.3.1. What is the chief source of information for printed monographs?

2.3.2. What do you use if there is no title page?

2.3.3. What does *prescribed source of information* mean?

2.3.4. Are you given specific rules for inscribing inaccuracies in a bibliographic record for a book?

2.3.5. Are most statements used in punctuation given in terms following or preceding the various types of information?

2.3.6. For what type of materials is the colophon considered the chief source of information?

2.3.7. What is the prescribed source of information for the physical description of an item?

2.3.8. For which 2.0x rules would you go to Chapter 1?

Part II Introduction

Part II of the *Anglo-American Cataloguing Rules*, 2nd edition, 1988 revision, contains specific information on choice of access points, headings, uniform titles, and references. These sections will help you learn to create headings and uniform titles in the proper format.

The rules deal with the choice of access points for main and added entries, form of personal and corporate name headings, geographic entries, uniform titles, and references. The chapter on references will apply to the authority control section as well, as it deals with *See*, *See Also*, and explanatory references. As in Part I, general rules precede special rules, and general rules apply where no specific rules exist.

Read the introductions (Rules 20.1–20.4, 21.0, 23.1, and 25.1) for more information on these topics.

2.4. Personal Authors (Chapter 22) Exercises

The following names have been found on items being cataloged by your library. Formulate them correctly according to *AACR2R* and give the rule you used as a guide.

2.4.1. Miss Read, pseudonym of Agnes Marie Saint.

AACR2R rule: ______________________________

____

2.4.2. By Grandfather Weeks.

AACR2R rule: ______________________________

____

2.4.3. For Myrtle by Cousin Belle.

AACR2R rule: ______________________________

____

2.4.4. Written by D. de F.

AACR2R rule: ______________________________

____

2.4.5. By Pliny the Elder.

AACR2R rule: ______________________________

____

2.4.6. Saint Augustine, Bishop of Hippo.

AACR2R rule: ______________________________

____

2.4.7. Poetry by Cecil Day-Lewis.

AACR2R rule: ______________________________

____

2.4.8. Story by Prince Philip.

AACR2R rule: ______________________________

____

2.4.9. The story of Alexander the Great, who lived from 356 to 323 B.C., in his own words.

AACR2R rule: ______________________________

____

2.4.10. Adventures in murder: the story of Dame Agatha Christie.

AACR2R rule: ______________________________

____

2.4.11. The greatest poet who ever lived: Baron George Gordon Byron.

AACR2R rule: ______________________________

____

2.4.12. By Marcus Tullius Cicero.

AACR2R rule: ______________________________

____

2.4.13. Maria Tall Chief.

AACR2R rule: ______________________________

____

2.4.14. Sir George Brown *[Knight]*

AACR2R rule: ______________________________

____

2.4.15. Pope Leo the Thirteenth

AACR2R rule: ______________________________

____

2.4.16. H.G. Wells

AACR2R rule: ______________________________

____

2.4.17. Buckskin Bill *[Television personality]*

AACR2R rule: ______________________________

____

2.4.18. Allen Stewart Konigsberg

AACR2R rule: ______________________________

____

2.4.19. Barbara Michaels

AACR2R rule: ______________________________

____

2.4.20. Hilda Doolittle

AACR2R rule: ______________________________

____

2.4.21. Suleiman the Magnificent

AACR2R rule: ______________________________

____

2.4.22. Prince Franz Joseph, of Hohenzollern

AACR2R rule: ______________________________

____

2.4.23. Frank MacDonald

AACR2R rule: ________________________________

____

2.4.24. Dr. Seuss

AACR2R rule: ________________________________

____

2.4.25. John Smith *[Ship captain]*

AACR2R rule: ________________________________

____

2.5. Corporate Bodies (Chapter 24), Exercise Set 1

The following corporate bodies have been found on items you are cataloging for your library collection. Use the *AACR2R* rule given, and formulate the names correctly.

2.5.1. Commission on Certification of Social Workers, Department of Health and Hospitals, Health and Social Rehabilitation Services Administration, State of Alabama.
AACR2R rule: 24.19

____

2.5.2. First Presbyterian Church of Boise, Idaho.
AACR2R rule: 24.10B

____

2.5.3. Commonwealth of Montana.
AACR2R rule: 24.3E

____

2.5.4. Third Governor's Conference on Mental Disabilities held in Ames, Iowa in 1957.
AACR2R rule: 24.7B

____

2.5.5. Coastal Resources Section, University of Mississippi.
AACR2R rule: 24.13

____

2.5.6. Pope Leo XIII *[Served from 1878; written under authority of his position within the Catholic Church]*
AACR2R rule: 24.17B2

____

2.5.7. State Committee of Louisiana's Republican Party.
AACR2R rule: 24.16A

____

2.5.8. West Baton Rouge Genealogical Society.
AACR2R rule: 24.1A1

____

2.5.9. Grand Lodge of Lafayette of the Ancient and Honorable Order of Freemasons.
AACR2R rule: 24.9A

____

2.5.10. Subcommittee on the Federal-Aid Adult Daycare Program, Committee on Public Health of the House of Representatives, United States Government.
AACR2R rule: 24.21C

____

____

____

2.5.11. Supreme Court of the State of Nebraska.
AACR2R rule: 24.23A

____

2.5.12. Technical Services Interest Group, Maine Library Association.
AACR2R rule: 24.13

____

2.5.13. U.S.S. Kidd.
AACR2R rule: 24.5C4

____

2.5.14. University of New Orleans, Architectural Students Forum.
AACR2R rule: 24.4C7

____

2.5.15. Mississippi's Pearl River Administration.
AACR2R rule: 24.18

____

2.5.16. Society of Jesus.
AACR2R rule: 24.3D1

____

2.5.17. Western Louisiana Diocese of the Episcopal Church.
AACR2R rule: 24.27C2

____

2.5.18. Center for Louisiana Studies, University of Southwestern Louisiana.
AACR2R rule: 24.12

____

2.5.19. KEEL radio station, Shreveport, Louisiana.
AACR2R rule: 24.11

____

2.5.20. Assessor of Lake Providence, Louisiana.
AACR2R rule: 24.20C1

____

2.5.21. National Council of the Presbyterian Church in America.
AACR2R rule: 24.27A1

____

2.5.22. Ironclad Monitor.
AACR2R rule: 24.4B

____

2.5.23. A Baptist church in Brooklyn named Holy Jesus Church.
AACR2R rule: 24.10

____

2.5.24. United States House of Representatives.
AACR2R rule: 24.21A

___

2.5.25. 16th Infantry Division of the American Army.
AACR2R rule: 24.24A1

___

2.5.26. Naval Air Corps of the United States.
AACR2R rule: 24.24A1

___

2.5.27. Louisiana's Constitutional Convention of 1989.
AACR2R rule: 24.22B

___

2.5.28. Department of Revenue, State of Utah.
AACR2R rule: 24.18

___

2.5.29. Fifth Rice Festival held in Cameron, Louisiana.
AACR2R rule: 24.8

___

2.5.30. Red River Compact Administration, States of Louisiana and Texas.
AACR2R rule: 24.15A

___

2.5.31. Cheniere Caminada Delta Management Program, Grand Isle, Louisiana.
AACR2R rule: 24.17

___

2.5.32. American embassy in Chile.
AACR2R rule: 24.18

___

2.5.33. President Clinton.
AACR2R rule: 24.20B

___

2.5.34. Kaw Valley Film & Video Inc.
AACR2R rule: 24.5C1

____

Corporate Bodies (Chapter 24), Exercise Set 2

The following names have been found on items being cataloged by your library. Formulate them correctly according to the *AACR2R* rule needed. State which rule you used to formulate the heading.

2.5.35. Mayor of Port Allen, Louisiana.

AACR2R rule: ______________________________

____

2.5.36. WJBO radio station, Baton Rouge, Louisiana.

AACR2R rule: ______________________________

____

2.5.37. Terrebonne Genealogical Society.

AACR2R rule: ______________________________

____

2.5.38. U.S.S. Louisiana.

AACR2R rule: ______________________________

____

2.5.39. Center for Wetland Resources, LSU & A&M College. *[Published in 1996]*

AACR2R rule: ______________________________

____

2.5.40. Pope John Paul the Second. *[Elected in 1978; written under authority of his position within the Catholic Church]*

AACR2R rule: ______________________________

____

2.5.41. Republican Party in Louisiana.

AACR2R rule: ______________________________

____

2.5.42. State Committee of Louisiana's Democratic Party.

AACR2R rule: ______________________________

____

2.5.43. American Federation of Labor and Congress of Industrial Organizations.

AACR2R rule: ______________________________

____

2.5.44. Second Governor's Conference on Physical Disabilities held in New Orleans in 1978.

AACR2R rule: ______________________________

____

2.5.45. Special Subcommittee on the Federal-Aid Highway Program, Committee on Public Works of the House of Representatives, United States Government.

AACR2R rule: ______________________________

____

____

2.5.46. Mississippi's Environmental Protection Agency.

AACR2R rule: ______________________________

____

2.5.47. Grand Lodge of Baton Rouge of the Ancient Order of Freemasons.

AACR2R rule: ______________________________

____

2.5.48. LSU & A&M College, Paul M. Hebert Law Center.

AACR2R rule: ______________________________

____

2.5.49. University of New Orleans, Tiger Tales Club.

AACR2R rule: ______________________________

____

2.5.50. Louisiana Diocese of the Catholic Church.

AACR2R rule: ______________________________

____

2.5.51. Second Order of St. Francis.

AACR2R rule: ______________________________

____

2.5.52. Supreme Court of the State of Louisiana.

AACR2R rule: ______________________________

____

2.5.53. President Kennedy.

AACR2R rule: ______________________________

____

2.5.54. First Baptist Church, Big Wood, Louisiana.

AACR2R rule: ______________________________

____

2.5.55. Bureau of Environmental Health, Louisiana's Department of Health and Hospitals, Health and Social Rehabilitation Services Administration.

AACR2R rule: ______________________________

____

2.5.56. Army Air Corps of the United States.

AACR2R rule: ______________________________

____

2.5.57. F4 Phantom.

AACR2R rule: ______________________________

____

2.5.58. National Council of the Episcopal Church in America.

AACR2R rule: ______________________________

____

2.5.59. United States Senate.

AACR2R rule: ______________________________

____

2.5.60. A Catholic church in Manhattan named All Saints Church.

AACR2R rule: ______________________________

____

2.5.61. Louisiana's Constitutional Convention of 1973.

AACR2R rule: ______________________________

____

2.5.62. 25th Infantry Division of the American Army.

AACR2R rule: ______________________________

____

2.5.63. Third Shrimp Festival held in Houma, Louisiana.

AACR2R rule: ______________________________

____

2.5.64. Department of Culture, Recreation and Tourism, State of Louisiana.

AACR2R rule: ______________________________

____

2.5.65. Sabine River Compact Administration, States of Louisiana and Texas.

AACR2R rule: ______________________________

____

2.5.66. British embassy in Mongolia.

AACR2R rule: ______________________________

____

2.5.67. Kisatchie-Delta Regional Management Program, Alexandria, Louisiana.

AACR2R rule: ______________________________

____

2.5.68. Coronet Film & Video Inc.

AACR2R rule: ______________________

____

2.6. Geographic Names, Exercise Set 1

The following geographic names have been found on items you are cataloging for your library collection. Use the *AACR2R* rule given and formulate the names correctly.

2.6.1. Paris, France
AACR2R rule: 23.4A1

____

2.6.2. A subdivision in Shreveport, Louisiana, called Broadmoor
AACR2R rule: 23.4A1

____

2.6.3. Peking, China
AACR2R rule: 23.2B1

____

2.6.4. Helsingfors, Finland
AACR2R rule: 23.2B1

____

2.6.5. Ontario, Canada
AACR2R rule: 23.4C1

____

2.6.6. Canadian city of Fort Erie
AACR2R rule: 23.4C2

____

2.6.7. York, England
AACR2R rule: 23.4D2

____

2.6.8. Ulaanbaatar, Mongolia
AACR2R rule: 23.4E

____

2.6.9. The town of Linwood, Georgia, in Bartow County
AACR2R rule: 23.4F1

____

2.6.10. The town of Linwood, Georgia in Walker County
AACR2R rule: 23.4F1

____

2.6.11. Kansas City, Missouri
AACR2R rule: 23.5A

____

Geographic Names, Exercise Set 2

To answer the following questions, formulate the place name according to *AACR2R*, and give the rule you used to create the name. You will probably need to use a gazetteer as well as *AACR2R*.

2.6.12. A town in Canada called Yellow Creek

AACR2R rule: ______________________________

____

2.6.13. Bonn, Germany

AACR2R rule: ______________________________

____

2.6.14. The port of Mendes in Brazil

AACR2R rule: ______________________________

____

2.6.15. The town of Strathaven

AACR2R rule: ______________________________

____

2.6.16. Queensland, Australia

AACR2R rule: ______________________________

____

2.6.17. Beijing, China

AACR2R rule: ______________________________

____

2.6.18. The Australian town of Alice Springs

AACR2R rule: ______________________________

____

2.6.19. Lhasa, Tibet

AACR2R rule: ______________________________

____

2.6.20. The new city of Laredo in Mexico

AACR2R rule: ______________________________

____

2.6.21. Bushmills, Northern Ireland

AACR2R rule: ______________________________

____

2.6.22. The U.S.-dependent territory of the Virgin Islands

AACR2R rule: ______________________________

____

2.6.23. Puerta Vallarta, Mexico

AACR2R rule: ______________________________

____

2.6.24. Omaha, Nebraska

AACR2R rule: ______________________________

____

2.6.25. Kathmandu, Nepal

AACR2R rule: ______________________________

____

2.6.26. The Welsh town of Llanelly

AACR2R rule: ______________________________

____

2.6.27. The town of Hidalgo in Mexico

AACR2R rule: ______________________________

____

2.6.28. Yukon Territory

AACR2R rule: ______________________________

____

2.7. Choice of Access Points

Access points are entries allowing access to information in a bibliographic record. Main author, title proper, uniform title, subject headings, and added entries are all examples of access points. Manual, or card catalog, systems need a main entry heading in order for all the works of a person to be filed together. A computer can find all the works of a person regardless of where the information is located—in a main entry, added entry, or series entry field, for example. Decisions about whether a name should be a main entry or added entry are perhaps less important for automated library systems, but contemporary practice requires that the decisions be made. This chapter will help you make decisions about those problem areas where there isn't a simple (one author, one title) choice of access points. This workbook discusses the rules in Chapter 21 dealing with text; rules dealing with nonprint materials are discussed in the *Cataloging Nonprint Materials* workbook in the Blitz Cataloging Workbook Series.

Choice of Access Points Exercises

Read the introductory rules for Chapter 21 and answer the following questions about choice of access points.

2.7.1. Explain what the rules in this chapter determine, as given in Rule 21.0A1.

2.7.2. What determines the access points for the item being cataloged?

2.7.3. What four terms can be appended to an added entry heading for a person?

2.7.4. Are these terms noted in full, or abbreviated?

2.7.5. Are these the only terms that can be added?

2.7.6. According to Rule 21.1A1, define *personal author*.

2.7.7. Which rule defines the use of a corporate body as main entry?

2.7.8. Define *emanate* as used in Rule 21.1B2.

2.7.9. What should you do if you are in doubt about whether a work falls into one or more of the categories in Rule 21.1B2?

2.7.10. What should you do if a work emanates from one or more corporate bodies and falls outside the categories given in Rule 21.1B2?

2.7.11. Is a work ever entered under title main entry? If so, when?

2.7.12. If a word in the title of a second edition of a work changes from "and" to "&", is it considered a new title?

2.7.13. What should you do if you are in doubt as to whether the title has changed?

2.7.14. Should you make a separate entry for a serial when the title changes, or just note the change and use the same record?

2.7.15. If a corporate body issuing a serial changes its name, but the serial title remains the same, should you make a new record, or just note the change and use the same record?

2.7.16. How would an official communication from a head of state be entered?

2.7.17. How would a presidential inaugural address be entered?

2.7.18. How should you enter a work whose identification of authorship consists of symbols?

2.7.19. Define *works of shared responsibility.*

2.7.20. When should you make a title main entry even if the item being cataloged has authors?

2.7.21. In the case of question 2.7.20, how many of the authors are given in the statement of responsibility? How many of these authors are traced as added entries?

2.7.22. In a work of joint authorship of two persons, which is given as the main entry?

2.7.23. In a collection of letters between two persons, which is given as the main entry?

2.7.24. If the names of joint authors appear in different order on the first and second editions of a work, how are the headings given for each work?

2.7.25. Whose name is used as main entry when two or more persons collaborate and use a single pseudonym?

2.7.26. What would be the main entry of a work that is a modification of another work?

2.7.27. What would be the main entry of a work that is an abridgement or rearrangement of another work?

2.7.28. What would be the main entry of a paraphrase, rewriting, adaptation for children, or version in a different literary form?

2.7.29. What would be the main entry for a translation of a work?

2.7.30. What should you do in any of the cases in 2.7.26, 2.7.27, 2.7.28, or 2.7.29 if you are in doubt?

2.7.31. Why are added entries necessary?

2.7.32. What types of information can be found in added entries?

2.7.33. Must a person or corporate body be named in the descriptive part of a bibliographic record before being included as an added entry?

2.7.34. Must all persons or corporate bodies named in the descriptive part of a bibliographic record be put in added entries?

2.7.35. Should all items containing several named works (a collection of stories, a sound recording, or multiple plays, for example) have analytical entries?

2.7.36. Are the legislative enactments and decrees of a political jurisdiction, and the decrees of a chief executive having the force of law ever entered under personal name main entry?

2.8. Uniform Titles

A uniform title brings together all catalog entries for a work that appears under various titles in different editions, translations, adaptations, or mediums of expression. A uniform title also correctly identifies a work when the title being cataloged is different from the title by which a work is known.

Use of uniform titles is optional; although the rules in *AACR2R* are stated as instructions, their application in any particular library depends on the policy of the library. Use of uniform titles can vary from one library to another and can even vary within a single library.

Uniform Titles Exercises

Answer the following questions about uniform titles.

2.8.1. How is the uniform title differentiated from the main title on a catalog card?

2.8.2. How is the uniform title differentiated from the main title in an automated system?

2.8.3. Does a uniform title used as a main entry heading include square brackets?

2.8.4. How should you transcribe a uniform title that is written in nonroman script?

2.8.5. What is the order of preference in languages for works published simultaneously in different languages and under different titles, none of which is known to be the original language or title?

2.8.6. If there is no title in any of the languages in the table of preference, which title would you use?

2.8.7. If the library receives only one edition of the work referred to in questions 2.8.5 and 2.8.6, would you use its language as the uniform title?

2.8.8. If a work was originally written in classical Greek, what would you use for the uniform title?

2.8.9. How would you distinguish between a person or corporate body and an identical uniform title being used as a heading or reference? [Example: Charlemagne]

2.8.10. How would you distinguish between two identical titles that refer to different works?

2.8.11. Where would you indicate that the item being cataloged is in a different language from the original?

2.8.12. Would you do the same thing for a motion picture with subtitles in a different language?

2.8.13. How would you indicate that the language of the item is an early form of a modern language?

2.8.14. How would you indicate that the item being cataloged is in two languages, one of them the original language?

2.8.15. What would you do if neither of the languages is the original language?

2.8.16. What would you do if there are three languages in the work being cataloged?

2.8.17. How would you indicate that only part of a work, unnumbered or nonconsecutively numbered, is the item being cataloged?

2.8.18. What uniform title would you use for an item consisting of the complete works of a person?

2.8.19. What uniform title would you use for an item consisting of more than three, but not all, works of a person?

2.8.20. What uniform title would you use for an item consisting of the complete works of a person in one particular form?

2.8.21. What if none of the above is appropriate?

2.8.22. What would you use for a uniform title for a complete or partial collection of legislative enactments of a jurisdiction?

2.8.23. What would you use for a uniform title for a single legislative enactment?

2.8.24. What would you use for a uniform title for several different laws with the same title enacted by the same jurisdiction?

2.8.25. What would you use for a uniform title for a collection of treaties between two given parties?

2.8.26. What if the collection of treaties was between one party and several other parties?

2.8.27. What would you use for a uniform title for a sacred scripture?

2.8.28. What is the sequence in which specific parts of the Bible would be given in a uniform heading?

2.8.29. What would the uniform title be for a group of books of the Bible?

2.8.30. What is the uniform title for the Apocrypha?

2.8.31. What is the uniform title for a single selection commonly identified by its own title rather than its designation as part of the Bible, for example, The Lord's Prayer?

2.8.32. If an item consists of two biblical selections encompassed by two uniform titles, do you use both uniform titles?

2.8.33. What is the order for additions to uniform titles for language, date, version, and so on?

2.8.34. If the item being cataloged is not the complete item, where do you put the information on version, year, and so on?

2.8.35. What is the uniform title for a particular order, or a tractate or treatise, of the Talmud?

2.8.36. What reference authority would you consult for the form of the name of a particular order or tractate of the Mishnah or Tosefta?

2.8.37. How would you enter one of the four standard collections of Vedas?

3.
AUTHORITY CONTROL

Authority files represent records of decisions made about the manner in which rules have been interpreted. An authority file serves two principal purposes for the cataloger: it is a reference to which one turns to discover whether a precedent exists for a particular heading, and it provides guidance, either from context or by example, for the creation of a new heading. Authority files provide a logical organization of related topics and specific and direct access to a known topic through a single search.

If a heading is not to be used in more than one record, maintaining it in an authority file serves little purpose. One must, therefore, make a decision to authorize all headings on the premise that they will be used again, or wait until the second time a particular heading is used in a bibliographic record to do the authority work. The second option entails checking your bibliographic files for every heading, then your authority files to see if you have already created it, then either creating it or not. It seems that the first choice is less work!

Although most librarians agree that authority control is a very important element of any catalog, the time and cost required to maintain an authority file often cause it to be a low priority. Yet, it is essential if the catalog is to truly serve the needs of its users. Efficient searching by author and subject is impossible if headings are inconsistent and cross-references are not available. If, for instance, some bibliographic records use Mark Twain and others use Samuel Langhorne Clemens; if some use Moss—Louisiana and some use Spanish moss; if some use Elephants and others use Pachyderms; if some use Neftali Reyes and others use Pablo Neruda, a search will retrieve only part of the library's holdings. A properly maintained authority file provides a consistent system of *See From* and *See Also* references that will yield more productive search results.

Authority control identifies the established form for headings for persons, corporate bodies, geographical names, uniform titles, series titles, subject headings of all types including topical, and any combination of these. It provides the reasons for the particular heading chosen, and for alternate forms of the heading, terms used previously, and broader, narrower, and/or related terms. Uniform headings (not uniform titles) provide an efficient means of finding all works for a person, a corporate body, and so forth. They allow patrons to find all items by or about a given author or subject without having to guess how the term will be entered. This also entails background work by the cataloger, who uses an established authority file for headings, such as *Library of Congress Subject Headings* or the OCLC authority file database. Authority files can be found in machine-readable form in an integrated library system, or in a separate manual card file. Both formats are discussed in this section.

The authority database is rarely available to the public. Patrons will be aware only of the *See From* and *See Also* references helping them find the correct heading.

3.1. Format of Authority Records

The *Format for MARC Authority Data* contains the official rules and requirements for creating authority files.

The 008 field gives coded data which is usually repeated in text form somewhere in the authority record. Each byte in the coded string is identified as a particular piece of information, and includes type of data, romanization scheme, type of government agency, type of series, series number, record update in process code, reference evaluation code, status of authority heading code, authority reference record code, undifferentiated personal name code, encoding level, modified record code, subject heading system code, and geographic subdivision code. For actual codes and more complete information, see the *Format for MARC Authority Data.*

The established heading is the main entry of an authority record. In an automated file it is found in a 1xx field: a personal name is entered in a 100 tag, a corporate entry in a 110 tag, a topical subject heading in a 150 tag, and so on. The 1xx field is not repeatable. In a manual file, the established heading is given at the top of the card. See the examples following this section.

See From references are variant forms of a heading suppressed in favor of the one that has been established as the authorized form. They are found in 4xx fields. This field is repeatable. These headings may include variant spellings of the authorized term, canceled (obsolete or pre-*AACR*) terms, other forms of names, pseudonyms, transliterated terms, acronyms, fuller/lesser hierarchical names, inverted forms, and more. In a manual file, *See From* references are designated with a single "x" or with UF [i.e., *Use For*]. More than one *See From* reference may be used in any given authority record.

See Also terms are variant forms of a heading which may also be used. They are found in 5xx fields, also repeatable. These headings may be earlier/later forms of corporate names, broader terms, related terms, or narrower terms. When a *See Also* reference is included, it must also be created as a 1xx tag. Both headings must have individual authority records. In a manual file, *See Also* references are designated with "xx" or as BT [*Broader Term*], NT [*Narrower Term*], RT [*Related Term*], or SA [*See Also*].

Series authorities are designed to include series treatment information as well as information concerning the heading. Information about the beginning and/or ending dates of publication and/or the volume designation of a series is found in a 640 field.

The 641 field is used for numbering peculiarities. This field contains unformatted notes citing report-year coverage or irregularities and peculiarities in numbering.

Source notes are found in 670 fields. The first 670 field is always the item being cataloged, which is the source of the name or term being authorized. 670 fields can also include other authorities, such as dictionaries, gazetteers, encyclopedias, and other published reference works, used for alternate forms of the established term. Phone calls to, and letters from, the author or publisher may also be cited. The 670 field is repeatable, and a record often has several sources, especially if there is a large number of *See From* and *See Also* references. When personal authors have their works translated into foreign languages, the translated forms of the name are often included as *See From* references, with the source of the translated name given in additional 670 fields. In a manual file, source notes follow the *See From* and *See Also* references.

Historical notes are used to give fuller information about previous forms of a heading such as the *AACR1* form of a name or the complex name changes typical of government agencies. These notes are found in a 667 field. Only one 667 field is used.

Epitome notes are found in a 678 field. They are used to record biographical or other information, such as profession, birthplace, or date a firm was established. This note is usually used only when converting manual files to machine-readable files. After manual files have been completed, the epitome note is incorporated into a 670 field.

Subject scope notes are used to give more information about the usage of the heading, usually referring to related or overlapping headings. These notes usually record scope notes as they appear in *LCSH*. In automated files, this note is found in a 680 field. In a manual file, the scope note follows the source notes.

The examples below show a MARC record and a manual authority card.

Rec stat:	Entered: 19950317		
Type: z	Upd status: a	Enc lvl: n	Source: d
Roman:	Ref status: a	Mod rec:	Name use: b
Govt agn:	Auth status: a	Subj: a	Subj use: a
Series: n	Auth/ref: a	Geo subd: I	Ser use: b
Ser num: n	Name: n	Subdiv tp:	Rules: n

040		≠a LSL ≠c LSL
110	20	≠a Pern Transportation Company.
410	10	≠a Pern. ≠b Transportation Co.
510	20	≠a Pernese Transport.
670		≠a Lilcamp, Jayge. Pern's premiere hauling service, 4562: p.5 (Pern Transportation Company; organized in 4537 as Pernese Transport, name changed in 4559)

Pern Transportation Company

UF Pern. Transportation Company.
SA Pernese Transport.

Lilcamp, Jayge. Pern's premiere hauling service, 4562: p.5 (Pern Transportation Company; organized in 4537 as Pernese Transport, name changed in 4559)

Rec stat:	Entered: 19950317		
Type: z	Upd status: a	Enc lvl: n	Source: d
Roman:	Ref status: a	Mod rec:	Name use: b
Govt agn:	Auth status: a	Subj: a	Subj use: a
Series: n	Auth/ref: a	Geo subd: I	Ser use: b
Ser num: n	Name: n	Subdiv tp:	Rules: n

040	≠a LSL ≠c LSL
151 0	≠a Vieux Carré (New Orleans, La.)
451 0	≠a French Quarter (New Orleans, La.)
551 0	≠a New Orleans (La.)
670	≠a Smith, James John. History of the Vieux Carré, 1993: ≠b p.1 (Vieux Carré, part of New Orleans, also called the French Quarter)

Vieux Carré (New Orleans, La.)

UF French Quarter (New Orleans, La.)
BT New Orleans (La.)

Smith, James John. History of the Vieux Carré, 1993: (Vieux Carré, part of New Orleans, also called the French Quarter)

Rec stat:	Entered: 19950317		
Type: z	Upd status: a	Enc lvl: n	Source: d
Roman:	Ref status: a	Mod rec:	Name use: a
Govt agn:	Auth status: a	Subj: a	Subj use: a
Series: n	Auth/ref: a	Geo subd: n	Ser use: b
Ser num: n	Name: n	Subdiv tp:	Rules: c

040		≠a LSL ≠c LSL
151	0	≠a Mongolia.
451	0	≠a MNR.
451	0	≠a Mongolia People's Republic.
451	0	≠a Mongol Uls.
451	0	≠a Bugd Nayramdah Mngol Ard Uls.
451	0	≠a Outer Mongolia.
451	0	≠a Mongolia, Outer.
551	0	≠a Inner Mongolia (China)

Mongolia

UF	MNR
	Mongolia People's Republic
	Mongol Uls
	Bugd Nayramdah Mngol Ard Uls
	Outer Mongolia
	Mongolia, Outer
RT	Inner Mongolia (China)

Rec stat:	Entered: 19950317		
Type: z	Upd status: a	Enc lvl: n	Source: d
Roman:	Ref status: a	Mod rec:	Name use: a
Govt agn:	Auth status: a	Subj: a	Subj use: a
Series: n	Auth/ref: a	Geo subd: n	Ser use: b
Ser num: n	Name: n	Subdiv tp:	Rules: c

040		≠a LSL ≠c LSL
130	00	≠a Bible. ≠p N.T. ≠p John.
430	00	≠a Bible. ≠p John.
430	00	≠a John (Book of the New Testament)

Bible. N.T. John.

UF Bible. John.
John (Book of the New Testament)

Rec stat:	Entered: 19950317		
Type: z	Upd status: a	Enc lvl: n	Source: d
Roman:	Ref status: a	Mod rec:	Name use: a
Govt agn:	Auth status: a	Subj: a	Subj use: a
Series: n	Auth/ref: a	Geo subd: n	Ser use: b
Ser num: n	Name: n	Subdiv tp:	Rules: c

Tag	Ind	Field
040		≠a DLC ≠c DLC ≠d DLC
100	0	≠a John, ≠c the Apostle, Saint.
400	0	≠a Jean, ≠c aptre, Saint.
400	0	≠a John, ≠c Saint, apostle.
500	0	≠a Beloved Disciple.
670		≠a Hieronymus. Lives of Matthew, Mark, Luke and John, c1896.
670		≠a Avril, M. Saint-Jean, aptre de la Sainte Eucharistie, 1982: ≠b t.p. (Saint-Jean, aptre)
670		≠a Grassi, J.A. The secret identity of the Beloved Disciple, 1990, c1989: ≠b CIP galley (Beloved Disciple, purported author of Gospel of John; traditionally identified with John the Apostle, but author disagrees)

John, the Apostle, Saint

UF Jean, aptre, Saint
John, Saint, apostle
RT Beloved Disciple

Hieronymus. Lives of Matthew, Mark, Luke and John, c1896.

Avril, M. Saint-Jean, aptre de la Sainte Eucharistie, 1982: t.p. (Saint-Jean, aptre)

Grassi, J.A. The secret identity of the Beloved Disciple, 1990, c1989; CIP galley (Beloved Disciple, purported author of Gospel of John; traditionally identified with John the Apostle, but author disagrees)

3.2. References

The examples below are a guide to be used to complete the exercises that follow them. They contain an abbreviated MARC format followed by a brief manual form. The exercises are to be completed using both manual and MARC formats.

Personal names, *See From* references

1. To the established name from another form of the name

   100 1 Smith, J. R. ≠q (John Robert)
   400 1 Smith, John Robert.

   Smith, J. R. (John Robert)
   UF Smith, John Robert

2. To established name from married/maiden name

   100 1 Smith, Mary Ann Harris.
   400 1 Harris, Mary Ann.

   Smith, Mary Ann Harris
   UF Harris, Mary Ann

3. To/from established name from/to a pseudonym, where only one is established

   100 1 Twain, Mark.
   400 1 Clemens, Samuel Langhorne.

   Twain, Mark
   UF Clemens, Samuel Langhorne

4. To established compound-surname from other forms

   100 1 Garcia Lorca, Carlos.
   400 1 Lorca, Carlos Garcia.

   Garcia Lorca, Carlos
   UF Lorca, Carlos Garcia

5. To established name from different forms of transliteration

   100 1 Evtushenko, Evgenii.
   400 1 Yevtushenko, Yevgenii.

   Evtushenko, Evgenii
   UF Yevtushenko, Yevgeni

Personal names, *See Also* references

(Used primarily when an author has established more than one persona, and uses them in authoring various types or genres of material.)

1. To pseudonyms from real name and/or other pseudonyms

    100 1 Mertz, Barbara.
    500 1 Michaels, Barbara.
    500 1 Peters, Elizabeth.

    Mertz, Barbara.
    SA Michaels, Barbara
    SA Peters, Elizabeth

Corporate names, *See From* references

1. To established name from acronyms

    110 2 Joint Council on Cataloging
    410 2 JCC.
    410 2 J.C.C.

    Joint Council on Cataloging
    UF JCC
    UF J.C.C.

2. To established name from fuller hierarchical name

    110 1 Louisiana. ≠b Office of State Parks.
    410 1 Louisiana. ≠b Department of Culture, Recreation and Tourism. ≠b Office of State Parks.

    Louisiana. Office of State Parks.
    UF Louisiana. Department of Culture, Recreation and Tourism. Office of State Parks

3. To established form from shorter form

    110 1 New Jersey. ≠b Department of Education. ≠b Music Section.
    410 1 New Jersey. ≠b Music Section.

    New Jersey. Department of Education. Music Section
    UF New Jersey. Music Section

4. To established form from unauthorized form which may be frequently found in publications

    110 1 New Mexico. ≠b Office of State Fire Marshal.
    410 1 New Mexico. ≠b State Fire Marshal.

    New Mexico. Office of State Fire Marshal
    UF New Mexico. State Fire Marshal

5. To established form from inverted form, to facilitate searching

   110 1 Rhode Island. ≠b Office of State Inspector General.
   410 1 Rhode Island. ≠b State Inspector General, Office of.

   Rhode Island. Office of State Inspector General
   UF Rhode Island. State Inspector General, Office of

Corporate names, *See Also* references

(Used especially with government agencies whose names have changed through reorganization, although private industry is not immune from this, either. Some governmental bodies have gone through a succession of name changes, and will therefore have several *See Also* references to reflect this history.)

1. To later form from earlier form of name

   110 2 State Library of Louisiana.
   510 2 Louisiana State Library.

   State Library of Louisiana
   SA Louisiana State Library

2. To earlier form from later form of name

   110 2 Louisiana State Library.
   510 2 State Library of Louisiana.

   Louisiana State Library
   SA State Library of Louisiana

Subject headings, *See From* references

(Makes your catalog much more user-friendly. Points the way from an unused term, a canceled heading, a different spelling; may turn frustration into smiles. These headings are also classed as *Use For* headings in current *LCSH* volumes.)

1. To established form from former headings that are obsolete

   150 0 Afro-Americans.
   450 0 Negroes.

   Afro-Americans
   UF Negroes

2. To established form from an unused heading

   150 0 Teenagers.
   450 0 Adolescents.

   Teenagers
   UF Adolescents

3. To established form from different spelling

   150 0 Teenagers.
   450 0 Teen-agers.

   Teenagers
   UF Teen-agers

Subject headings, *See Also* references

(Help point the user to other terms that may be useful in a search.)

1. To established form from broader terms

   150 0 Tigers.
   550 0 Mammals.

   Tigers
   BT Mammals

2. To established form from narrower terms

   150 0 Iris.
   550 0 Louisiana iris.

   Iris
   NT Louisiana iris

3. To established form from another similar topic

   150 0 Underpasses.
   550 0 Subways.

   Underpasses
   SA Subways

Geographical names, *See From* references

1. To established form from non-authorized form

   151 0 Latin America.
   451 0 Spanish America.

   Latin America
   UF Spanish America

2. To established form from earlier name

   151 0 Russia, Northern.
   451 0 Soviet Union, Northern.

   Russia, Northern
   UF Soviet Union, Northern

3. To established form from abbreviation

   151 0 Saint Helens, Mount (Wash.)
   451 0 St. Helens, Mount (Wash.)

   Saint Helens, Mount (Wash.)
   UF St. Helens, Mount (Wash.)

4. To established form from former, unauthorized form

   151 0 Louisiana.
   451 0 Louisiane.

   Louisiana
   UF Louisiane

5. To established form from non-ISBD forms that were previously used for the term

   151 0 Red River Parish (La.)
   451 0 Red River Parish, La.

   Red River Parish (La.)
   UF Red River Parish, La.

Geographical names, *See Also* references

1. To established form from broader term

   151 0 Vieux Carré (New Orleans, La.)
   551 0 New Orleans (La.)

   Vieux Carré (New Orleans, La.)
   BT New Orleans (La.)

2. To established form from related term

   151 0 New York Metropolitan Area.
   551 0 New York Suburban Area.

   New York Metropolitan Area
   RT New York Suburban Area

3. To established form from narrower term

   151 0 Nigeria ≠x History.
   551 0 Senussite Rebellion, 1916-1918.

   Nigeria--History
   NT Senussite Rebellion, 1916-1918

References Exercises

Create *See From* or *See Also* references for the following terms. Use both automated and manual forms. Use correct tagging. You may need to verify 4xx and 5xx fields by using other sources such as *LCSH*, *Sears List of Subject Headings*, *AACR2R*, gazetteers, and other reference works. The term in parentheses is the form to be provided.

Personal names, *See From* references

3.2.1. (Another form of the name)

100 1 Jones, Seymour R. ≠q (Seymour Rochambaud)
400 1 ______________________________

Jones, Seymour R. (Seymour Rochambaud)

____

3.2.2. (Real name)

100 1 Brand, Max.

____

Brand, Max

____

3.2.3. (Single surname)

100 1 Hendricks Boynton, Janice.

____

Hendricks Boynton, Janice

____

3.2.4. (Maiden name)

100 1 Brown, Katherine Rice

____

Brown, Katherine Rice

____

Personal names, *See Also* references

3.2.5. (Pseudonym)

100 1 Dodgson, Charles Lutwidge, ≠d 1832–1898.

____

Dodgson, Charles Lutwidge, ≠d 1832–1898

____

Corporate names, *See From* references

3.2.6. (Fuller hierarchical name)

110 1 Louisiana. ≠b Office of State Library.

Louisiana. Office of State Library

3.2.7. (Shorter hierarchical name)

110 1 Kentucky. ≠b Department of Education. ≠b Vocational Education Section.

Kentucky. Department of Education. Vocational Educational Section.

3.2.8. (Acronym)

110 2 Bureau of National Affairs

Bureau of National Affairs.

3.2.9. (Inverted form)

110 1 United States. ≠b Department of the Interior.

United States. Department of the Interior

Corporate names, *See Also* references

3.2.10. (Later form of name)

110 2 Louisiana State University and Agricultural and Mechanical College.

Louisiana State University and Agricultural and Mechanical College

---

3.2.11. (Earlier form of name)

110 2 Newcomb College.

Newcomb College

Subject headings, *See From* references

3.2.12. (Different spelling)
150 0 Babysitting.

Babysitting

3.2.13. (Obsolete heading)
150 0 Gay men.

Gay men

3.2.14. (Unused heading)
150 0 Police.

Police

Subject headings, *See Also* references

3.2.15. (Similar topic)
150 0 Cookery, American ≠x Louisiana style.

Cookery, American--Louisiana style

3.2.16. (Narrower topic)
150 0 Reptiles.

Reptiles

3.2.17. (Broader topic)
150 0 Cherokee Indians.

Cherokee Indians

3.2.18. (Related topic)

150 0 Elevators.

Elevators

Geographical names, *See From* references

3.2.19. (Earlier form of the name)

151 0 Kola Peninsula (Russia)

Kola Peninsula (Russia)

3.2.20. (Abbreviation)

151 0 Saint John the Baptist Parish (La.)

Saint John the Baptist Parish (La.)

3.2.21. (Non-ISBD form)

151 0 Cobb County (Ga.)

Cobb County (Ga.)

3.2.22. (Former, unauthorized form)

151 0 Pennsylvania.

Pennsylvania

Geographical names, *See Also* references

3.2.23. (Related term)

151 0 Washington D.C. Metropolitan Area.

Washington D.C. Metropolitan Area

3.2.24. (Narrower term)

151 0 New Orleans (La.) ≠x History.

New Orleans (La.)--History

3.2.25. (Broader term)

151 0 Manhattan (New York, N.Y.)

Manhattan (New York, N.Y.)

3.3. Authority Control

Authority Control, Exercise Set 1

Decide the correct main entry and any cross-reference entries (*Use For, See Also, Narrower Terms, Broader Terms,* and *Related Terms*) that would be applicable and create the appropriate authority record. Add a source note.

3.3.1. Lawnmower repairs
Source: Ferguson, Gary. Repairing your power lawnmower, c1992.

1__ _ _ ≠a ______________________

4__ _ _ ≠a ______________________

4__ _ _ ≠a ______________________

5__ _ _ ≠a ______________________

670 ≠a ______________________

____

____

3.3.2. Mount Driskoll
Source: Lilly, Joyce. Louisiana's highest peak, c1991.

1__ _ _ ≠a ______________________

4__ _ _ ≠a ______________________

4__ _ _ ≠a ______________________

5__ _ _ ≠a ______________________

670 ≠a ______________________

____

____

3.3.3. Thomas Francis Jaques
Source: Jaques, Thomas F. Autobiography of a State Librarian, c2001 (Thomas F. Jaques, nickname Tom, p. ii).

1__ _ _ ≠a ______________________________

4__ _ _ ≠a ______________________________

4__ _ _ ≠a ______________________________

5__ _ _ ≠a ______________________________

670 ≠a ______________________________

____

____

3.3.4. Louisiana governor's office
Source: State of the state report, 1995, 1995 (Louisiana Office of the Governor--t.p.).

1__ _ _ ≠a ______________________________

4__ _ _ ≠a ______________________________

4__ _ _ ≠a ______________________________

5__ _ _ ≠a ______________________________

670 ≠a ______________________________

____

____

3.3.5. Gideon Oliver
Source: Elkins, Aaron. The dark place, 1987 (also known as Professor Oliver and the Skeleton Detective).

1__ _ _ ≠a ______________________________

4__ _ _ ≠a ______________________________

4__ _ _ ≠a ______________________________

5__ _ _ ≠a ______________________________

670 ≠a ______________________________

____

____

3.3.6. Marvin W. (Trey) Lewis, III
Source: Lewis, Marvin Wells. Indian artifacts of the Gulf Coast, c1998 (phone call to author: generally known as Trey; he was born in 1964).

1__ _ _ ≠a ______________________________

4__ _ _ ≠a ______________________________

4__ _ _ ≠a ______________________________

5__ _ _ ≠a ______________________________

670 ≠a ______________________________

____

____

008 (Header) Information, Authority Control

Authority records, like bibliographic records, contain an 008 field which consists of coded data about the record. The information, however, deals with specifics such as romanization scheme, type of series, type of government document, and whether it is a subject heading or an author heading. There are forty bytes (00–39), each with a specific meaning. The codes below will help you fill out the header for authority records and complete the given exercises.

00–05—Date entered on file. Formatted as *yymmdd* (year/year/month/month/day/day).

06—Direct or indirect geographic subdivision; indicates whether the 1xx heading may be subdivided geographically when used as a subject heading and, if so, the method of subdivision used.

—(Blank) Not geographically subdivided
d—Subdivided geographically—direct
i—Subdivided geographically—indirect
n —Not applicable

07—Romanization scheme; indicates whether the 1xx field contains the romanized form of the heading and, if so, the romanization scheme used.

a—International standard
b—National standard
c—National library association standard
d—National library or bibliographic agency standard
e—Local standard
f— Standard of unknown origin
g—Conventional romanization or conventional form of name in language of cataloging agency
n—Not applicable; the 1xx heading is not romanized

08—Language of catalog; indicates whether the heading in the 1xx field and its associated reference structure are valid according to the rules used in establishing heading for English-language catalogs, French-language catalogs, or both.

—No information provided
b—English and French
e—English only
f—French only

09—Kind of record; indicates whether the record represents an established or unestablished 1xx heading.

a—Established heading
b—Untraced reference; not traced as a 4xx field in any established heading record
c—Traced reference; contains an unestablished heading that is traced as a 4xx field in the record
d—Subdivision; unestablished heading that may be used as a subject subdivision
e—Node label
f—Established heading and subdivision; an established heading that may be used as a main term and as a subject subdivision
g—Reference and subdivision; unestablished heading that may be used as a reference term and as a subject division

10—Descriptive cataloging rules

a—Earlier rules; cataloging conventions used prior to *AACR1*
b—*AACR1*
c—*AACR2*
d—*AACR2*-compatible heading
n—Not applicable
z—Other

11—Subject heading system/thesaurus

a—Library of Congress Subject Headings
b—LC subject headings for children's literature
c—Medical Subject Headings (MeSH)
d—National Agricultural Library subject authority file
k—Canadian Subject Headings
n—Not applicable
r—Art and Architecture Thesaurus
s—Sears List of Subject Headings
v—Repertoire des vedettes-matiere
z—Other

12—Type of series
- a—Monographic
- b—Multipart item
- c—Series-like phrase
- d—Not applicable
- z—Other

13—Numbered or unnumbered series
- a—Numbered
- b—Unnumbered
- c—Numbering varies
- n—Not applicable

14—Heading use—main or added entry
- a—Appropriate
- b—Not appropriate

15—Heading use—subject added entry
- a—Appropriate
- b—Not appropriate

16—Heading use—series added entry
- a—Appropriate
- b—Not appropriate

17—Type of subject subdivision
- a—Topical
- b—Form
- c—Chronological
- d—Geographic
- e—Language
- n—Not applicable

18–27—Undefined
- —(Blank)

28—Type of government agency
- —(Blank)—Not a government agency
- a—Autonomous or semi-autonomous
- c—Multilocal
- f— Federal/national
- i—International
- l—Local
- m—Multistate
- o—Government agency, type undetermined

s—State, provincial, etc.
u—Unknown if heading is a government agency or not
z—Other

29—Reference evaluation; indicates whether the 4xx/5xx tracing fields in a record have been evaluated for consistency with the rules used to formulate the 1xx heading
a—Tracings consistent with heading
b—Tracings not necessarily consistent with heading
n—Not applicable

30—Undefined
—(Blank)

31—Record update in process code
a—Record can be used
b—Record being updated; do not use

32—Undifferentiated personal name; indicates whether a personal name heading is used by one person or by two or more persons
a—Differentiated personal name
b—Undifferentiated personal name
n—Not applicable

33—Level of establishment
a—Fully established
b—Memorandum; heading is fully established but has not been used in a bibliographic record
c—Provisional; heading cannot be formulated satisfactorily because of inadequate information
d—Preliminary; heading taken from a bibliographic record because the bibliographic item was not available at the time the heading was established
n—Not applicable

34–37—Undefined
—(Blank)

38—Modified record code
—(Blank)—Not modified
s—Shortened
x—Missing characters; characters that could not be converted into machine-readable form due to character set limitations are missing from the record

39—Cataloging source
—(Blank)—National bibliographic agency
c—Cooperative cataloging program
d—Other
u—Unknown

Authority Control, Exercise Set 2

Use the codes given previously to create 008 tags (fixed field information) from the information given in each record. Use the date you create the information, in the form of *yymmdd* [year/year/month/month/day/day]; i.e., August 5, 1997, would be coded 970805. Some positions in the 008 field will be blank.

3.3.7.	008		. . . .
	100	10	≠a Sharp, Sam H., ≠d 1943-
	400	10	≠a Sharp, Samuel Harelson, ≠d 1943-
	670		≠a His Exercise by mail delivery, 1996: ≠b t.p. (Sam H. Sharp); p. ii (born Samuel Harelson Sharp, Jr. in 1943)
	670		≠a Letter from author: (Prefers to be known as Sam H. Sharp)

3.3.8.	008		. . . .
	100	10	≠a Sharp, Sam H., ≠d 1967-
	400	10	≠a Sharp, Samuel Harelson, ≠d 1967-
	670		≠a His Programming made easy, 1998: ≠b t.p. (Sam H. Sharp, III); p. ii (born Samuel Harelson Sharp, III in 1967)
	670		≠a Letter from author: (Prefers to be known as Sam H. Sharp)

3.3.9.	008		. . . .
	100	10	≠a Finley, Betty Jo.
	400	10	≠a Finley, Elizabeth Josephine.
	670		≠a Her Cataloging for demonstration libraries, 1972: ≠b t.p. (Betty Jo Finley; t.p. verso Elizabeth Josephine Finley)
	670		≠a Letter from author: (Prefers Betty Jo Finley)

3.3.10.	008		. . . .
	100	10	≠a Wilde, Oscar, ≠d 1854-1900.
	400	10	≠a Wilde, Oscar Fingall O'Flahertie Wills, ≠d 1854-1900.
	400	10	≠a C. 3. 3., ≠d 1854–1900.
	670		≠a His The letters, c1962: ≠b p. 3 (b. 16 Oct. 1854; 26 Apr. 1855 christened)
	670		≠a Montgomery Hyde, H. Oscar Wilde, c1975: ≠b p.6 (b. 16 Oct. 1854; several biogr. and encyc. articles, incl. Dict. of natl. biog., wrongly state b. 16 Oct. 1856; error seems arisen from his vanity in habitually understating his age; date of b. placed beyond doubt by his baptismal record, which is still in existence)
	670		≠a Halkett & Laing: ≠b v.1, p. 172 (C.3.3. [Oscar Wilde])
	670		≠a His Children in prison... 1898 ≠b (hdg.: Wilde, Oscar, 1854-1900; variant: Oscar Fingall O'Flahertie Wills Wilde)

3.3.11. 008 . . . .
100 10 ≠a Cartwright, George, ≠d 1739-1819.
400 00 ≠a G. C. ≠q (George Cartwright), ≠d 1739-1819.
400 10 ≠a C., G. ≠q (George Cartwright, ≠d 1739-1819.
670 ≠a His A journal of transactions and events, ... 1792: ≠b t.p. (George Cartwright, Esq.)

3.3.12. 008 . . . .
100 10 ≠a Mather, Cotton, ≠d 1663-1728.
400 00 ≠a English minister, ≠d 1663-1728.
670 ≠a His A memorial of the present deplorable state of N.E.: ≠b (Cotton Mather)
670 ≠a His An epistle to the Christian Indians ... 1700: ≠b t.p. (an English minister)

3.3.13. 008 . . . .
100 00 ≠a James ≠b I, ≠c King of England, ≠d 1566-1625.
400 00 ≠a James ≠b VI, ≠c King of Scotland, ≠d 1566-1625.
400 00 ≠a James ≠b I, ≠c King of Great Britain, ≠d 1566-1625.

3.3.14. 008 . . . .
100 10 ≠a Clinton, Bill, ≠d 1946-
400 10 ≠a Clinton, William J. ≠q (William Jefferson), ≠d 1946-
400 10 ≠a Blythe, William Jefferson, ≠d 1946–
510 10 ≠a Arkansas. ≠b Governor (1979-1981 : Clinton)
510 10 ≠a Arkansas. ≠b Governor (1983-1992 : Clinton)
510 10 ≠a United States. ≠b President (1993- : Clinton)
670 ≠a His Summary of exec. recommend. for the budget, State of Ark., FY 1980-81, 1981?: ≠b t.p. (Bill Clinton, governor)
670 ≠a Washington Post, 21 Jan. 1993: ≠b (William Jefferson Clinton elected 42nd President of the United States)

3.3.15. 008 . . . .
110 20 ≠a West Baton Rouge Parish Library.
410 10 ≠a West Baton Rouge Parish (La.). ≠b Library.
550 0 ≠a Public libraries ≠z Louisiana ≠z Port Allen.
670 ≠a Boyce, Judy. Three Frog Night, c1996: ≠b t.p. (West Baton Rouge Parish Library, Port Allen, Louisiana)

3.3.16. 008 . . . .
110 20 ≠a Saint James Episcopal Church (Baton Rouge, La.)
410 20 ≠a St. James Episcopal Church (Baton Rouge, La.)
410 10 ≠a Baton Rouge (La.). ≠b Saint James Episcopal Church.
550 0 ≠a Episcopal church ≠z Louisiana ≠z Baton Rouge.
670 ≠a Its One hundred years at Saint James, 1995: ≠b t.p. (Saint James Episcopal Church, Baton Rouge, Louisiana)

3.3.17. 008 . . . .

110 20 ≠a Columbia Pictures.

410 20 ≠a Columbia Pictures Industries. ≠b Columbia Pictures.

670 ≠a Silverado [MP], 1985: ≠b credits (Columbia Pictures)

670 ≠a LC data base, 10-9-86 ≠b (hdg.: Columbia Pictures)

670 ≠a International motion picture almanac, 1983 ≠b (Columbia Pictures Corporation was incorporated in 1/10/24. In 12/28/68 Columbia Pictures Corporation was reorganized as Columbia Pictures Industries, Inc. with Columbia Pictures as a major division)

3.3.18. 008 . . . .

110 20 ≠a American Telephone and Telegraph Company.

410 20 ≠a A. T. & T.

410 20 ≠a Bell Telephone System.

410 20 ≠a American Telephone & Telegraph Company.

410 20 ≠a AT&T.

510 20 ≠a American Bell Telephone Company.

670 ≠a Its Annual report, 1900.

670 ≠a Wasserman, N. From invention to innovation, c1985: ≠b CIP galley (AT & T: American Telephone and Telegraph Company)

670 ≠a LC manual auth. cd. ≠b (hdg.: American Bell Telephone Company; organized 1880; merged 1900 in the American Telephone and Telegraph Company which had originally been formed, 1885, by the American Bell Telephone Company to build and operate its long distance system)

3.3.19. 008 . . . .

110 20 ≠a National Air and Space Museum.

410 20 ≠a Smithsonian Institution. ≠b National Air and Space Museum.

410 10 ≠a United States. ≠b National Air and Space Museum.

410 20 ≠a Smithsonian Air and Space Museum.

410 10 ≠a Washington (D.C.). ≠b National Air and Space Museum.

410 20 ≠a Air and Space Museum (U.S.)

510 20 ≠a National Air Museum (U.S.)

670 ≠a Dickey, P.S. The Liberty engine, 1918-1942, 1968.

3.3.20. 008 . . . .

110 20 ≠a International Brotherhood of Teamsters, Chauffeurs, Warehousemen and Helpers of America.

410 20 ≠a Chauffeurs, International Brotherhood of.

410 20 ≠a Warehousemen, International Brotherhood of.

410 20 ≠a International Teamsters Union.

410 20 ≠a Teamsters Union.

410 20 ≠a IBT.

510 20 ≠a International Brotherhood of Teamsters.

670 ≠a NUCMC data: ≠b (International Brotherhood of Teamsters, Chauffeurs, Warehousemen and Helpers of America)

670 Teamsters all, 1976: ≠b (International Brotherhood of Teamsters, Chauffeurs, Stablemen and Helpers; in 1940, at the Teamster convention in Washington, DC, the word "Warehousemen" was officially substituted for the word "Stablemen" in the title of the organ., International Brotherhood of Teamsters, Chauffeurs, Warehousemen and Helpers of America)

670 ≠a Its Official magazine, Nov. 1910: cover (International Brotherhood [of] Teamsters, Chauffeurs, Stablemen and Helpers of America) ; ≠a The New Teamster, Sept. 1992: t.p. verso (International Brotherhood of Teamsters)

3.3.21. 008 . . . .

110 20 ≠a National Baseball Hall of Fame and Museum.

410 20 ≠a National Baseball Museum (Cooperstown, N.Y.)

410 20 ≠a Hall of Fame (Baseball Museum : Cooperstown, N.Y.)

410 10 ≠a Cooperstown (N.Y.). ≠b National Baseball Hall of Fame and Museum.

670 ≠a National Baseball Museum, inc. Hall of Fame ... c1942.

3.3.22. 008 . . . .

110 20 ≠a University of Alabama.

410 10 ≠a Alabama. ≠b University.

410 10 ≠a Alabama. ≠b University of Alabama.

410 20 ≠a Alabama University.

667 ≠a AACR1 form: University of Alabama.

670 ≠a Its Catalogue of the officers and students of the University of Alabama, session of ... 1874-'75: ≠b t.p. (University of Alabama)

670 The Alabama University monthly, Nov. 1874: ≠b t.p. (Alabama University)

3.3.23. 008 . . . .
150 0 ≠a Enriched cereal products.
450 0 ≠a Cereal products, Enriched.
450 0 ≠a Fortified cereal products.
550 0 ≠a Cereal products.
550 0 ≠a Enriched foods.
670 ≠a Smith, Judith. Sources for fortified cereals, c1997.

3.3.24. 008 . . . .
150 0 ≠a Iran-Contra Affair, 1985–1990.
450 0 ≠a Contra-Iran Affair, 1985–1990.
450 0 ≠a Contragate, 1985–1990.
450 0 ≠a Iran-Contra Arms Scandal, 1985–1990.
450 0 ≠a Irangate, 1985–1990.
550 0 ≠a Military assistance, American ≠z Iran.
550 0 ≠a Military assistance, American ≠z Nicaragua.
550 0 ≠a Political corruption ≠z United States.
551 0 ≠a United States ≠x Politics and government ≠y 1981-1989.
670 ≠a South, Olive. Oh, what tales..., 1993

3.3.25. 008 . . . .
150 0 ≠a Teuso languages.
450 0 ≠a Kuliak languages.
550 0 ≠a Nilo-Saharan languages.
551 0 ≠a Uganda ≠x Languages.
670 ≠a Tsingeng, Baharu. Aspects of the Teuso languages, c1994.

3.3.26. 008 . . . .
150 0 ≠a Smock family.
450 0 ≠a Smack family.
450 0 ≠a Smak family.
450 0 ≠a Smoke family.
450 0 ≠a Smook family.
550 0 ≠a Schmucker family.
670 ≠a Smoke, Jan. Smoke, Smook, and Smack get in your eyes, c1995.

3.3.27. 008 . . . .
151 0 ≠a Badlands Wilderness (Or.)
451 0 ≠a Badlands Wilderness Study Area (Or.)
550 0 ≠a National parks and reserves ≠z Oregon.
550 0 ≠a Wilderness areas ≠z Oregon.
670 ≠a Rancher, Buddy. Badlands as bad lands, c1987.

3.3.28.	008		. . . .
	150	0	≠a Country musicians.
	450	0	≠a Hillbilly musicians.
	550	0	≠a Musicians.
	550	0	≠a Bluegrass musicians.
	550	0	≠a Gospel musicians.
	550	0	≠a Women country musicians.
	670		≠a Tonesing, Ada. Music awards, c1987.

3.3.29.	008		. . . .
	150	0	≠a Palenque Indians.
	450	0	≠a Guarina Indians.
	450	0	≠a Palank Indians.
	450	0	≠a Palenca Indians.
	450	0	≠a Palenke Indians.
	550	0	≠a Indians of South America ≠z Venezuela.
	550	0	≠a Tamanac Indians.
	670		≠a Story of the Palanks: oral histories, c1992.

3.3.30.	008		. . . .
	150	0	≠a Matrix derivatives.
	450	0	≠a Derivatives, Matrix.
	550	0	≠a Functions.
	550	0	≠a Matrices.
	670		≠a Doctorow, Jonathan James. Matrix derivatives, c1992.

3.3.31.	008		. . . .
	130	00	≠a Time Life books your money matters
	410	20	≠a Time Life Books. ≠t Time Life Books your money matters
	430	00	≠a Your money matters (Alexandria, Va.)
	643		≠a Alexandria, VA ≠b Time-Life
	670		≠a Basics of investing, 1996: ≠b CIP t.p. (Time Life Books your money matters)

3.3.32.	008		. . . .
	130	00	≠a G.K. Hall large print book series
	430	00	≠a Hall large print book series
	430	00	≠a G.K. Hall large print series
	430	00	≠a Boston, Mass. ≠b G.K. Hall
	670		≠a Marshall, C. Julie, 1985, c1984: ≠b CIP t.p. verso

3.3.33.	008		. . . .
	130	00	≠a Social work practice with children and families
	643		≠a New York ≠b Guilford Press
	670		≠a Webb, N.B. Social work practice with children, 1996: ≠b CIP data sheet (Social work practice with children and families)

3.3.34. 008 . . . .
130 00 ≠a Social movements past and present
430 00 ≠a Social movements past & present
430 00 ≠a Twayne's social movements series
430 00 ≠a Twayne's social movements past and present
643 ≠a Boston, Mass. ≠b Twayne Publishers ≠d (1982-1991)

3.3.35. 008 . . . .
130 00 ≠a Bulletin (Louisiana. Dept. of Education)
410 10 ≠a Louisiana. ≠b Dept. of Education. ≠t Bulletin
410 10 ≠a Louisiana. ≠b Dept. of Education. ≠t Bulletin--Louisiana State Department of Education
643 ≠a Baton Rouge, LA (P.O. Box 44064, Baton Rouge, 70804) ≠b Printing Section, Dept. of Education.

3.3.36. 008 . . . .
130 00 ≠a Theatre Arts book
430 00 ≠a Theatre Arts books
430 00 ≠a Theater arts books
643 ≠a New York, N.Y. ≠b Routledge
667 ≠a Give as a quoted note if Theatre Arts Books does not appear in publication, etc., area
670 ≠a Rutter, C.C. Clamorous voices, c1988 (1989 printing): ≠b t.p. (A Theatre Arts book)

3.3.37. 008 . . . .
130 00 ≠a Lonely Planet travel survival kit
430 00 ≠a Travel survival kit
643 ≠a South Yarra, Vic., Australia ≠a Berkeley, CA, USA ≠b Lonely Planet publications

3.3.38. 008 . . . .
130 00 ≠a Johns Hopkins series in hematology/oncology
430 00 ≠a Series in hematology/oncology
430 00 ≠a Johns Hopkins series in hematology and oncology
643 ≠a Baltimore ≠b Johns Hopkins University Press
670 ≠a Cancer treatment and the heart, c1992: ≠b CIP data sheet (The Johns Hopkins series in hematology/oncology)
670 ≠a Phone call to pub., 4/17/92 ≠b (The Johns Hopkins series in hematology/oncology is unnumbered)

Authority Control, Exercise Set 3

Create an authority record for each of the following items. Use the information provided and, if necessary, consult *LCSH*, *Sears List of Subject Headings*, *AACR2R*, a gazetteer, or other reference works. You are given the term the way it appears on the item being cataloged, and it is not necessarily the way it is to be established, although it MAY be. The names in parentheses always come from the item to be cataloged, and may be used as the authorized heading and the *See From* and *See Also* references.

Each record must have a main entry, at least one *See From* reference or one *See Also* reference (some may have more than one of each), and at least one source note. If *See Also* references are made, another authority record for the *See Also* reference as a main heading MUST be made.

You must also give your record an 040 tag, with subfields ≠a and ≠c. The first subfield (≠a) identifies the creator of the record. Use your initials (first, middle, last) in the ≠a. The second subfield (≠c) tells the source of the authority. If you use Library of Congress as your authority (subject or name), code the ≠c as DLC. If you use *Sears List of Subject Headings* as your authority, code the ≠c as SSH. If you use your own judgment (i.e., create the authorized heading as you think it should be), code the ≠c with your initials (first, middle, last).

Write your answers on the templates provided on pages 111–127. If you use a 5xx field, you must make two authority records. Put the number of the term being authorized in the space given on the template; if you have two authority records for the item, both authority records should have the same number. Make a 670 field for *LCSH* where needed, with edition used, date, volume, and pages.

Corporate Names

3.3.39. Westin Photographic Company

Sources:

1. *Westin Professional Moving Pictures and Stills*, c1983 (Westin Photographic Company)
2. Smith, William Robert. *A Westin History*, c1993 (Westin Photographic Company; established in August 1901 as Westin Films; succeeded by Westin Photographs, 1918; Westin Photographic Company in 1935.) (The company began publishing in 1952.)

3.3.40. Louisiana State Department of Education

Sources:

1. La. Bureau of Minority Education. *End-of-the-year report for minority education programs, 1984* (Louisiana Dept. of Education; Louisiana State Dept. of Education)
2. Matt, Katherine. *Louisiana history*, 1966. (State Dept. of Public Education)

3.3.41. Minton-Shropshire Porcelain Co., Ltd.

Sources:

1. *Pseudo-porcelains*, 1895 (Minton-Shropshire Porcelain Company Limited)
2. William, Teal. *The history of the Minton and Shropshire Companies*, 1996 (Firm founded in 1832 as Minton-Shropshire Porcelain Company Limited; used "Minton Porcelain Company", "Shropshire Porcelain Company" and "M-SP" on various manufactures during 1835–1839; began again in 1840 using Minton-Shropshire Porcelain Co.)

3.3.42. National Library of Medicine
Sources:
1. U.S. Congress. Senate Committee on the Judiciary. *A National Library of Medicine: hearings*, 1956. (National Library of Medicine)
2. *Centenary of Index Medicus, 1879-1979*, 1980 (U.S. Dept. of Health and Human Services, Public Health Service, National Institutes of Health, National Library of Medicine)
3. *Index of NLM serial titles*, [1972]- (NLM)

3.3.43. PAR
Source:
1. *A PAR report, 1951* (Public Affairs Research Council of Louisiana, inc.) Note: Organized in 1950.

3.3.44. St. Boudreaux County Public Library
Source:
1. Majors, John B. *The end of the line*, c1975 (St. Boudreaux County Public Library)

3.3.45. Our Lady of the Mountains Undergraduate Library
Sources:
1. Marsh, Guinevere. *University of Guadalupe Libraries*, 1993 (Our Lady of the Mountains Undergraduate Library; OLM Library)
2. Sangria, Maria. *Holdings in the OLM Library*, 1988 (OLM Library; Our Lady Undergraduate Library; Our Lady of the Mountains Undergraduate Library)

3.3.46. US3, Irish rock group
Sources:
1. *Cedar trees of heaven* [SR], 1984 (US3)
2. Smith, Jim. "US 3 have made it big in the U.S.", *Newsweekly*, Aug. 15, 1997 (US3; Us Three)

Geographic Names

3.3.47. Cape of Good Hope, South Africa [*the land mass, not the city*]
Source:
1. Jarreau, Parkinson. *Touring the Cape and the vineyards*, 1991 (Cape Peninsula)

3.3.48. Bay of Cartagena in Colombia
Source:
1. Willow, Diego. *A multisensory picture of Cartagena Bay, Colombia*, 1982 (Cartagena Bay)

3.3.49. Karana, the ancient city in Iraq
Source:
1. Killeen, Sheila. *El Souk and Karana*, c1976 (Karana, Iraq)

3.3.50. England's Lake District
Source:
1. Marsh, Inde. *Touring the Lake District*, 1994.

3.3.51. Gulf of Mexico
Source:
1. Lockout, Clyde. *The Gulf of Mexico*, 1973.

3.3.52. Mississippi Valley
Source:
1. Halley, B.T. *Big Father of Waters*, 1989 (Mississippi River; Mississippi Valley)

3.3.53. Lake Pontchartrain
Source:
1. Jones, Billy Bob. *Lake Pontchartrain*, c1954.

3.3.54. Middle fork of the Salmon River, Idaho
Source:
1. Zines, Winfred. *Middle Fork of the Salmon*, c1980.

Personal Names

3.3.55. Mickey W
Sources:
1. *The Autobiography of Mickey W*, 1978 (Mickey W; b. 1942, d. 1970)
2. *Encyclopedic dictionary of African-Americans*, c1975 (Mickey W, born 1/1/42, d. 2/2/70; b. as Michael Jones; also known as Big Al Mullins)

3.3.56. Governor Jimmie Davis
Sources:
1. *Louisiana, here I come!* 1963 (Jimmie Davis)
2. Davis, Jimmie. *You are my sunshine*, 1985 (James Houston Davis, b. 9/11/02; governor of Louisiana 1944-1948, 1960-1964; preferred to be known as Jimmie)

3.3.57. John Huey
Sources:
1. His *The extraneous murders*, 1923.
2. *Contemptuous Authors*, v. 1195 (b. 3/29/1874, d. 8/28/1969; b. as Charles John Huey Smith)
Also writes as Charles Smith.

3.3.58. Vincent-Willem van Gogh
Sources:
1. *Tableaux, aquarelles, dessin...* 1904 (Vincent van Gogh)
2. *Vincent van Gogh (1853-1890)*, 1958 (Vincent-Willem van Gogh, b. 3/30/1853, d. 7/29/1890)

3.3.59. Carolyn Lambert-Pitcherly
Sources:
1. *First you must make the roux*, by Carolyn Lambert-Pitcherly, c1991.
2. *Great Chefs of the South*, 1995 (Carolyn Lambert Pitcherly)

3.3.60. Susan L. Bentley
Sources:
1. *Avoyelles Parish, the happy parish*, by Susan L. Bentley, c1979.
2. Lewis, M. L., III. *Coushatta and the Indians*, c1994 (Sue Bentley)

3.3.61. Donald Henry Bartholomew
Sources:
1. *Don Bartholomew's Mongolia*, c1996.
2. Phone call to author, 5/16/96: full name is Donald Henry Bartholomew; born in Ulaanbaatar, Mongolia, on 1/25/63; usage: Don Bartholomew

3.3.62. Mrs. Humphry Ward
Sources:
1. *Helbeck of Bannisdale*, 1883, by Mrs. Humphry Ward (b. Mary Augusta Arnold; in Hobart, Tasmania, in 1851)
2. *Oxford companion to English literature*, 1985 (Mary Augusta Ward; d. 1920)

Topical Subject Headings

3.3.63. Coats of arms
Source:
1. Brault, G. J. *Early blazon*, c1972.

3.3.64. Catahoula hounds
Source:
1. Jenkins, Huey. *Encyclopedia of the Catahoula hound*, c1992.
2. Brown, W.C. *The Catahoula hog dog*, c1962.

3.3.65. Exhaustion, Mental
Source:
1. Green, W.J. *Fatigue free*, c1992.
2. Ferguson, Bobby. *How to catalog with joy*, c1999.

3.3.66. Growing roses
Source:
1. Baker, M.L. *Roses and their culture*, c1991.

3.3.67. Pedigreed Rhodesian ridgeback dogs
Source:
1. Linzy, J. *Rhodesian ridgeback champions, 1955-1980*, c1981.
2. Sewell, Joseph T. *Hounds of the world*, c1975.

3.3.68. Christian theology
Source:
1. Montefiore, H. *Credible Christianity*, c1994.

3.3.69. Garlands
Source:
1. Pflumm, C.C. *Hearthstrings*, c1993.

3.3.70. Painting with acrylic paints
Source:
1. Taubes, F. *Acrylic painting for the beginner*, c1971.

TEMPLATES

No.____

008
040 ≠a______ ≠c______
1_ _ _ _ ≠a______
4_ _ _ _ ≠a______
4_ _ _ _ ≠a______
5_ _ _ _ ≠a______
5_ _ _ _ ≠a______
670 ≠a______
670 ≠a______

No.____

008
040 ≠a______ ≠c______
1_ _ _ _ ≠a______
4_ _ _ _ ≠a______
4_ _ _ _ ≠a______
5_ _ _ _ ≠a______
5_ _ _ _ ≠a______
670 ≠a______
670 ≠a______

No.____

008
040 ≠a______ ≠c______
1_ _ _ _ ≠a______
4_ _ _ _ ≠a______
4_ _ _ _ ≠a______
5_ _ _ _ ≠a______
5_ _ _ _ ≠a______
670 ≠a______
670 ≠a______

No._____

008
040 ≠a_______ ≠c_______
1_ _ _ _ ≠a____
4_ _ _ _ ≠a____
4_ _ _ _ ≠a____
5_ _ _ _ ≠a____
5_ _ _ _ ≠a____
670 ≠a____
670 ≠a____

No._____

008
040 ≠a_______ ≠c_______
1_ _ _ _ ≠a____
4_ _ _ _ ≠a____
4_ _ _ _ ≠a____
5_ _ _ _ ≠a____
5_ _ _ _ ≠a____
670 ≠a____
670 ≠a____

No._____

008
040 ≠a_______ ≠c_______
1_ _ _ _ ≠a____
4_ _ _ _ ≠a____
4_ _ _ _ ≠a____
5_ _ _ _ ≠a____
5_ _ _ _ ≠a____
670 ≠a____
670 ≠a____

No._____

008
040 ≠a_______ ≠c_______
1_ _ _ _ ≠a____
4_ _ _ _ ≠a____
4_ _ _ _ ≠a____
5_ _ _ _ ≠a____
5_ _ _ _ ≠a____
670 ≠a____
670 ≠a____

No.______

008
040 ≠a________ ≠c________
1_ _ _ _ ≠a______________________________
4_ _ _ _ ≠a______________________________
4_ _ _ _ ≠a______________________________
5_ _ _ _ ≠a______________________________
5_ _ _ _ ≠a______________________________
670 ≠a______________________________
670 ≠a______________________________

No.______

008
040 ≠a________ ≠c________
1_ _ _ _ ≠a______________________________
4_ _ _ _ ≠a______________________________
4_ _ _ _ ≠a______________________________
5_ _ _ _ ≠a______________________________
5_ _ _ _ ≠a______________________________
670 ≠a______________________________
670 ≠a______________________________

No.______

008
040 ≠a________ ≠c________
1_ _ _ _ ≠a______________________________
4_ _ _ _ ≠a______________________________
4_ _ _ _ ≠a______________________________
5_ _ _ _ ≠a______________________________
5_ _ _ _ ≠a______________________________
670 ≠a______________________________
670 ≠a______________________________

No.______

008
040 ≠a________ ≠c________
1_ _ _ _ ≠a______________________________
4_ _ _ _ ≠a______________________________
4_ _ _ _ ≠a______________________________
5_ _ _ _ ≠a______________________________
5_ _ _ _ ≠a______________________________
670 ≠a______________________________
670 ≠a______________________________

No._____

008
040 ≠a_______ ≠c_______
1_ _ _ _ ≠a____
4_ _ _ _ ≠a____
4_ _ _ _ ≠a____
5_ _ _ _ ≠a____
5_ _ _ _ ≠a____
670 ≠a____
670 ≠a____

No._____

008
040 ≠a_______ ≠c_______
1_ _ _ _ ≠a____
4_ _ _ _ ≠a____
4_ _ _ _ ≠a____
5_ _ _ _ ≠a____
5_ _ _ _ ≠a____
670 ≠a____
670 ≠a____

No._____

008
040 ≠a_______ ≠c_______
1_ _ _ _ ≠a____
4_ _ _ _ ≠a____
4_ _ _ _ ≠a____
5_ _ _ _ ≠a____
5_ _ _ _ ≠a____
670 ≠a____
670 ≠a____

No._____

008
040 ≠a_______ ≠c_______
1_ _ _ _ ≠a____
4_ _ _ _ ≠a____
4_ _ _ _ ≠a____
5_ _ _ _ ≠a____
5_ _ _ _ ≠a____
670 ≠a____
670 ≠a____

No._____

008
040 ≠a_______ ≠c_______
1_ _ _ _ ≠a____
4_ _ _ _ ≠a____
4_ _ _ _ ≠a____
5_ _ _ _ ≠a____
5_ _ _ _ ≠a____
670 ≠a____
670 ≠a____

No._____

008
040 ≠a_______ ≠c_______
1_ _ _ _ ≠a____
4_ _ _ _ ≠a____
4_ _ _ _ ≠a____
5_ _ _ _ ≠a____
5_ _ _ _ ≠a____
670 ≠a____
670 ≠a____

No._____

008
040 ≠a_______ ≠c_______
1_ _ _ _ ≠a____
4_ _ _ _ ≠a____
4_ _ _ _ ≠a____
5_ _ _ _ ≠a____
5_ _ _ _ ≠a____
670 ≠a____
670 ≠a____

No._____

008
040 ≠a_______ ≠c_______
1_ _ _ _ ≠a____
4_ _ _ _ ≠a____
4_ _ _ _ ≠a____
5_ _ _ _ ≠a____
5_ _ _ _ ≠a____
670 ≠a____
670 ≠a____

No._____

008
040 ≠a_______ ≠c_______
1_ _ _ _ ≠a________________
4_ _ _ _ ≠a________________
4_ _ _ _ ≠a________________
5_ _ _ _ ≠a________________
5_ _ _ _ ≠a________________
670 ≠a________________
670 ≠a________________

No._____

008
040 ≠a_______ ≠c_______
1_ _ _ _ ≠a________________
4_ _ _ _ ≠a________________
4_ _ _ _ ≠a________________
5_ _ _ _ ≠a________________
5_ _ _ _ ≠a________________
670 ≠a________________
670 ≠a________________

No._____

008
040 ≠a_______ ≠c_______
1_ _ _ _ ≠a________________
4_ _ _ _ ≠a________________
4_ _ _ _ ≠a________________
5_ _ _ _ ≠a________________
5_ _ _ _ ≠a________________
670 ≠a________________
670 ≠a________________

No._____

008
040 ≠a_______ ≠c_______
1_ _ _ _ ≠a________________
4_ _ _ _ ≠a________________
4_ _ _ _ ≠a________________
5_ _ _ _ ≠a________________
5_ _ _ _ ≠a________________
670 ≠a________________
670 ≠a________________

No._____

008
040 ≠a_______ ≠c_______
1_ _ _ _ ≠a_______________
4_ _ _ _ ≠a_______________
4_ _ _ _ ≠a_______________
5_ _ _ _ ≠a_______________
5_ _ _ _ ≠a_______________
670 ≠a_______________
670 ≠a_______________

No._____

008
040 ≠a_______ ≠c_______
1_ _ _ _ ≠a_______________
4_ _ _ _ ≠a_______________
4_ _ _ _ ≠a_______________
5_ _ _ _ ≠a_______________
5_ _ _ _ ≠a_______________
670 ≠a_______________
670 ≠a_______________

No._____

008
040 ≠a_______ ≠c_______
1_ _ _ _ ≠a_______________
4_ _ _ _ ≠a_______________
4_ _ _ _ ≠a_______________
5_ _ _ _ ≠a_______________
5_ _ _ _ ≠a_______________
670 ≠a_______________
670 ≠a_______________

No._____

008
040 ≠a_______ ≠c_______
1_ _ _ _ ≠a_______________
4_ _ _ _ ≠a_______________
4_ _ _ _ ≠a_______________
5_ _ _ _ ≠a_______________
5_ _ _ _ ≠a_______________
670 ≠a_______________
670 ≠a_______________

No._____

008
040 ≠a_______ ≠c_______
1_ _ _ _ ≠a______________________________
4_ _ _ _ ≠a______________________________
4_ _ _ _ ≠a______________________________
5_ _ _ _ ≠a______________________________
5_ _ _ _ ≠a______________________________
670 ≠a______________________________
670 ≠a______________________________

No._____

008
040 ≠a_______ ≠c_______
1_ _ _ _ ≠a______________________________
4_ _ _ _ ≠a______________________________
4_ _ _ _ ≠a______________________________
5_ _ _ _ ≠a______________________________
5_ _ _ _ ≠a______________________________
670 ≠a______________________________
670 ≠a______________________________

No._____

008
040 ≠a_______ ≠c_______
1_ _ _ _ ≠a______________________________
4_ _ _ _ ≠a______________________________
4_ _ _ _ ≠a______________________________
5_ _ _ _ ≠a______________________________
5_ _ _ _ ≠a______________________________
670 ≠a______________________________
670 ≠a______________________________

No._____

008
040 ≠a_______ ≠c_______
1_ _ _ _ ≠a______________________________
4_ _ _ _ ≠a______________________________
4_ _ _ _ ≠a______________________________
5_ _ _ _ ≠a______________________________
5_ _ _ _ ≠a______________________________
670 ≠a______________________________
670 ≠a______________________________

No._____

008
040 ≠a_______ ≠c_______
1_ _ _ _ ≠a____
4_ _ _ _ ≠a____
4_ _ _ _ ≠a____
5_ _ _ _ ≠a____
5_ _ _ _ ≠a____
670 ≠a____
670 ≠a____

No._____

008
040 ≠a_______ ≠c_______
1_ _ _ _ ≠a____
4_ _ _ _ ≠a____
4_ _ _ _ ≠a____
5_ _ _ _ ≠a____
5_ _ _ _ ≠a____
670 ≠a____
670 ≠a____

No._____

008
040 ≠a_______ ≠c_______
1_ _ _ _ ≠a____
4_ _ _ _ ≠a____
4_ _ _ _ ≠a____
5_ _ _ _ ≠a____
5_ _ _ _ ≠a____
670 ≠a____
670 ≠a____

No._____

008
040 ≠a_______ ≠c_______
1_ _ _ _ ≠a____
4_ _ _ _ ≠a____
4_ _ _ _ ≠a____
5_ _ _ _ ≠a____
5_ _ _ _ ≠a____
670 ≠a____
670 ≠a____

No._____

008
040 ≠a_______ ≠c_______
1_ _ _ _ ≠a______________________________
4_ _ _ _ ≠a______________________________
4_ _ _ _ ≠a______________________________
5_ _ _ _ ≠a______________________________
5_ _ _ _ ≠a______________________________
670 ≠a______________________________
670 ≠a______________________________

No._____

008
040 ≠a_______ ≠c_______
1_ _ _ _ ≠a______________________________
4_ _ _ _ ≠a______________________________
4_ _ _ _ ≠a______________________________
5_ _ _ _ ≠a______________________________
5_ _ _ _ ≠a______________________________
670 ≠a______________________________
670 ≠a______________________________

No._____

008
040 ≠a_______ ≠c_______
1_ _ _ _ ≠a______________________________
4_ _ _ _ ≠a______________________________
4_ _ _ _ ≠a______________________________
5_ _ _ _ ≠a______________________________
5_ _ _ _ ≠a______________________________
670 ≠a______________________________
670 ≠a______________________________

No._____

008
040 ≠a_______ ≠c_______
1_ _ _ _ ≠a______________________________
4_ _ _ _ ≠a______________________________
4_ _ _ _ ≠a______________________________
5_ _ _ _ ≠a______________________________
5_ _ _ _ ≠a______________________________
670 ≠a______________________________
670 ≠a______________________________

No._____

008
040 ≠a_______ ≠c_______
1_ _ _ _ ≠a____
4_ _ _ _ ≠a____
4_ _ _ _ ≠a____
5_ _ _ _ ≠a____
5_ _ _ _ ≠a____
670 ≠a____
670 ≠a____

No._____

008
040 ≠a_______ ≠c_______
1_ _ _ _ ≠a____
4_ _ _ _ ≠a____
4_ _ _ _ ≠a____
5_ _ _ _ ≠a____
5_ _ _ _ ≠a____
670 ≠a____
670 ≠a____

No._____

008
040 ≠a_______ ≠c_______
1_ _ _ _ ≠a____
4_ _ _ _ ≠a____
4_ _ _ _ ≠a____
5_ _ _ _ ≠a____
5_ _ _ _ ≠a____
670 ≠a____
670 ≠a____

No._____

008
040 ≠a_______ ≠c_______
1_ _ _ _ ≠a____
4_ _ _ _ ≠a____
4_ _ _ _ ≠a____
5_ _ _ _ ≠a____
5_ _ _ _ ≠a____
670 ≠a____
670 ≠a____

No.____

008
040 ≠a_______ ≠c_______
1_ _ _ _ ≠a________________
4_ _ _ _ ≠a________________
4_ _ _ _ ≠a________________
5_ _ _ _ ≠a________________
5_ _ _ _ ≠a________________
670 ≠a________________
670 ≠a________________

No.____

008
040 ≠a_______ ≠c_______
1_ _ _ _ ≠a________________
4_ _ _ _ ≠a________________
4_ _ _ _ ≠a________________
5_ _ _ _ ≠a________________
5_ _ _ _ ≠a________________
670 ≠a________________
670 ≠a________________

No.____

008
040 ≠a_______ ≠c_______
1_ _ _ _ ≠a________________
4_ _ _ _ ≠a________________
4_ _ _ _ ≠a________________
5_ _ _ _ ≠a________________
5_ _ _ _ ≠a________________
670 ≠a________________
670 ≠a________________

No.____

008
040 ≠a_______ ≠c_______
1_ _ _ _ ≠a________________
4_ _ _ _ ≠a________________
4_ _ _ _ ≠a________________
5_ _ _ _ ≠a________________
5_ _ _ _ ≠a________________
670 ≠a________________
670 ≠a________________

No.______

008
040 ≠a________ ≠c________
1_ _ _ _ ≠a______________________________
4_ _ _ _ ≠a______________________________
4_ _ _ _ ≠a______________________________
5_ _ _ _ ≠a______________________________
5_ _ _ _ ≠a______________________________
670 ≠a______________________________
670 ≠a______________________________

No.______

008
040 ≠a________ ≠c________
1_ _ _ _ ≠a______________________________
4_ _ _ _ ≠a______________________________
4_ _ _ _ ≠a______________________________
5_ _ _ _ ≠a______________________________
5_ _ _ _ ≠a______________________________
670 ≠a______________________________
670 ≠a______________________________

No.______

008
040 ≠a________ ≠c________
1_ _ _ _ ≠a______________________________
4_ _ _ _ ≠a______________________________
4_ _ _ _ ≠a______________________________
5_ _ _ _ ≠a______________________________
5_ _ _ _ ≠a______________________________
670 ≠a______________________________
670 ≠a______________________________

No.______

008
040 ≠a________ ≠c________
1_ _ _ _ ≠a______________________________
4_ _ _ _ ≠a______________________________
4_ _ _ _ ≠a______________________________
5_ _ _ _ ≠a______________________________
5_ _ _ _ ≠a______________________________
670 ≠a______________________________
670 ≠a______________________________

No._____

008
040 ≠a_______ ≠c_______
1_ _ _ _ ≠a____
4_ _ _ _ ≠a____
4_ _ _ _ ≠a____
5_ _ _ _ ≠a____
5_ _ _ _ ≠a____
670 ≠a____
670 ≠a____

No._____

008
040 ≠a_______ ≠c_______
1_ _ _ _ ≠a____
4_ _ _ _ ≠a____
4_ _ _ _ ≠a____
5_ _ _ _ ≠a____
5_ _ _ _ ≠a____
670 ≠a____
670 ≠a____

No._____

008
040 ≠a_______ ≠c_______
1_ _ _ _ ≠a____
4_ _ _ _ ≠a____
4_ _ _ _ ≠a____
5_ _ _ _ ≠a____
5_ _ _ _ ≠a____
670 ≠a____
670 ≠a____

No._____

008
040 ≠a_______ ≠c_______
1_ _ _ _ ≠a____
4_ _ _ _ ≠a____
4_ _ _ _ ≠a____
5_ _ _ _ ≠a____
5_ _ _ _ ≠a____
670 ≠a____
670 ≠a____

No._____

008
040 ≠a_______ ≠c_______
1_ _ _ _ ≠a____
4_ _ _ _ ≠a____
4_ _ _ _ ≠a____
5_ _ _ _ ≠a____
5_ _ _ _ ≠a____
670 ≠a____
670 ≠a____

No._____

008
040 ≠a_______ ≠c_______
1_ _ _ _ ≠a____
4_ _ _ _ ≠a____
4_ _ _ _ ≠a____
5_ _ _ _ ≠a____
5_ _ _ _ ≠a____
670 ≠a____
670 ≠a____

No._____

008
040 ≠a_______ ≠c_______
1_ _ _ _ ≠a____
4_ _ _ _ ≠a____
4_ _ _ _ ≠a____
5_ _ _ _ ≠a____
5_ _ _ _ ≠a____
670 ≠a____
670 ≠a____

No._____

008
040 ≠a_______ ≠c_______
1_ _ _ _ ≠a____
4_ _ _ _ ≠a____
4_ _ _ _ ≠a____
5_ _ _ _ ≠a____
5_ _ _ _ ≠a____
670 ≠a____
670 ≠a____

No.____

008	
040	≠a____ ≠c____
1_ _ _ _	≠a____
4_ _ _ _	≠a____
4_ _ _ _	≠a____
5_ _ _ _	≠a____
5_ _ _ _	≠a____
670	≠a____
670	≠a____

No.____

008	
040	≠a____ ≠c____
1_ _ _ _	≠a____
4_ _ _ _	≠a____
4_ _ _ _	≠a____
5_ _ _ _	≠a____
5_ _ _ _	≠a____
670	≠a____
670	≠a____

No.____

008	
040	≠a____ ≠c____
1_ _ _ _	≠a____
4_ _ _ _	≠a____
4_ _ _ _	≠a____
5_ _ _ _	≠a____
5_ _ _ _	≠a____
670	≠a____
670	≠a____

No.____

008	
040	≠a____ ≠c____
1_ _ _ _	≠a____
4_ _ _ _	≠a____
4_ _ _ _	≠a____
5_ _ _ _	≠a____
5_ _ _ _	≠a____
670	≠a____
670	≠a____

No._____

008
040 ≠a_______ ≠c_______
1_ _ _ _ ≠a____
4_ _ _ _ ≠a____
4_ _ _ _ ≠a____
5_ _ _ _ ≠a____
5_ _ _ _ ≠a____
670 ≠a____
670 ≠a____

No._____

008
040 ≠a_______ ≠c_______
1_ _ _ _ ≠a____
4_ _ _ _ ≠a____
4_ _ _ _ ≠a____
5_ _ _ _ ≠a____
5_ _ _ _ ≠a____
670 ≠a____
670 ≠a____

No._____

008
040 ≠a_______ ≠c_______
1_ _ _ _ ≠a____
4_ _ _ _ ≠a____
4_ _ _ _ ≠a____
5_ _ _ _ ≠a____
5_ _ _ _ ≠a____
670 ≠a____
670 ≠a____

No._____

008
040 ≠a_______ ≠c_______
1_ _ _ _ ≠a____
4_ _ _ _ ≠a____
4_ _ _ _ ≠a____
5_ _ _ _ ≠a____
5_ _ _ _ ≠a____
670 ≠a____
670 ≠a____

BIBLIOGRAPHY

99% of being thought a genius consists
of knowing who to ask for information!

—Trey Lewis, Director
Red River Parish Library

General Materials

ALA Glossary of Library and Information Science. Chicago: American Library Association, 1982.

Chan, Lois Mai. *Cataloging and Classification: An Introduction.* 2nd ed. New York: McGraw-Hill, 1994.

Downing, Mildred Harlow, and David H. Downing. *Introduction to Cataloging and Classification.* 6th ed., rev. and greatly enlarged in accordance with *AACR2R88* and *DDC20*. Jefferson, N.C.: McFarland, 1992.

Intner, Sheila S., and Jean Weihs. *Standard Cataloging for School and Public Libraries.* 2nd ed. Englewood, Colo.: Libraries Unlimited, 1996.

Saye, Jerry D., and Desretta V. McAllister-Harper. *Manheimer's Cataloging and Classification: A Workbook.* 3rd ed., rev. and expanded. New York: Marcel Dekker, 1991.

Wynar, Bohdan S. *Introduction to Cataloging and Classification.* 8th ed. Arlene G. Taylor, ed. Englewood, Colo.: Libraries Unlimited, 1992.

Special Materials

Anglo-American Cataloguing Rules. 2nd ed., 1988 revision. Prepared under the direction of the Joint Steering Committee for Revision of AACR, a committee of: the American Library Association, the Australian Committee on Cataloguing, the British Library, the Canadian Committee on Cataloguing, the Library Association, the Library of Congress. Edited by Michael Gorman and Paul W. Winkler. Chicago: American Library Association, 1988.

Cundif, Margaret Fwelk. *Cataloging Concepts: Descriptive Cataloging, Instructor's Manual.* Matthew E. Gildea, ed. 2 vols. Washington, D.C.: Cataloging Distribution Service, Library of Congress, 1993.

Cutter, Charles Ammi. *Three-Figure Standard Cutter Table.* Chicopee Falls, Mass.: H.R. Hunting Company, n.d.

Library of Congress. Cataloging and Support Office. *Library of Congress Subject Headings.* 20th ed. Washington, D.C.: Library of Congress, 1997.

Library of Congress. *USMARC Format for Authority Data: Including Guidelines for Content Designation.* Washington, D.C.: Library of Congress, 1989– .

Millsap, Larry, and Terry Ellen Ferl. *Descriptive Cataloging for the AACR2R and USMARC: A How-To-Do-It Workbook.* New York: Neal-Schuman, 1991.

Sears List of Subject Headings. 16th ed. Joseph Miller, ed. New York: H.W. Wilson Co., 1997.

Periodicals and Serials

Cataloging & Classification Quarterly. Binghamton, N.Y.: Haworth Press, 1980– . Quarterly.

Cataloging Service Bulletin. Washington, D.C.: Library of Congress, 1978– . Quarterly.

Library Resources & Technical Services. Chicago: American Library Association, 1982– . Quarterly.

Technical Services Quarterly. Binghamton, N.Y.: Haworth Press, 1983– . Quarterly.

Technicalities. Kansas City, Mo.: Media Services Publications, 1981– . Monthly.

ANSWER KEY
DESCRIPTIVE CATALOGING

1.1. Families of Tags Exercise Answers

1.1.1. 6xx
1.1.2. 245
1.1.3. 4xx
1.1.4. 9xx
1.1.5. 1xx
1.1.6. 0xx
1.1.7. 8xx
1.1.8. 3xx
1.1.9. 7xx
1.1.10. 24x
1.1.11. 25x
1.1.12. 5xx
1.1.13. Locally defined fields
1.1.14. Computer utilization fields
1.1.15. Added entry fields
1.1.16. Title fields
1.1.17. Notes fields
1.1.18. Main entry fields
1.1.19. Series added entry fields
1.1.20. Edition and scale fields
1.1.21. Physical description fields
1.1.22. Subject heading fields
1.1.23. Series fields
1.1.24. Imprint field
1.1.25. Uniform title entry

1.1.26. Personal name

1.1.27. Conference or meeting name

1.1.28. Corporate body

1.1.29. x30

1.1.30. x10

1.1.31. x11

1.1.32. x00

1.2. 008 Field, Bibliographic Records, Exercise Set 1 Answers

1.2.1.
a. 440629
b. 860501
c. 641111
d. 890415
e. 960923
f. 780308

1.2.2.

a.	r	1997	1991
b.	m	1981	1987
c.	s	1997	
d.	c	1963	9999
e.	q	1970	1979
f.	q	1900	1950
g.	p	1973	1986
h.	n		

1.2.3.
a. mou
b. nju
c. aru
d. mdu
e. mau
f. flu
g. enk
h. fr
i. ch
j. vi
k. bn

1.2.4.
a. bfl
b. cdeg
c. a
d. hijk
e. aekl
f. agm
g. bde
h. acfh
i. cjp
j. bdg

1.2.5.
a. j
b. b
c. e
d. e
e. g
f. a
g. d
h. g
i. c
j. b

1.2.6.
a. b
b. f
c. a
d. d
e. c

1.2.7.
a. i
b. k
c. c
d. s
e. l
f. v
g. j
h. b

1.2.8.
a. l
b. f
c. s
d. i
e. ____
f. c
g. m

1.2.9.
a. a
b. c
c. c
d. b
e. d
f. ____

1.2.10.
a. fre
b. vie
c. eng
d. chi
e. spa
f. ger
g. ita
h. ara

1.2.11.
a. s
b. d
c. x
d. o
e. ____

1.2.12.
a. d
b. ____
c. n
d. d
e. c
f. d
g. a
h. d

1.2.13.	a.	G	Type of date/Publication status
	b.	M	Festschrift
	c.	G	Place of publication, production, or execution
	d.	M	Conference publication
	e.	G	Date entered on file
	f.	G	Language
	g.	M	Illustrations
	h.	G	Cataloging source
	i.	M	Nature of contents
	j.	G	Date 1
	k.	M	Undefined
	l.	G	Modified record
	m.	G	Date 2
	n.	M	Index
	o.	M	Government publication
	p.	M	Target audience
	q.	M	Biography
	r.	M	Form of item
	s.	M	Fiction

008 Field, Bibliographic Records, Exercise Set 2 Answers

```
1.2.14. 008   ......s1996....nyua.....b....001.0.eng.d
1.2.15. 008   ......s1997....nyu...........000.0.eng.d
1.2.16. 008   ......s1997....msuab....b....001.0.eng.d
1.2.17. 008   ......s1995....nyub..........001.0.eng.d
1.2.18. 008   ......s1996....ohuac....b....000.0.eng.d
1.2.19. 008   ......s1997....fr.ab....b....001.0.fre.d
1.2.20. 008   ......s1993....utuab.........001.0.eng.d
1.2.21. 008   ......s1997....ilu......b....001.0.eng.d
1.2.22. 008   ......s1997....enka..........000.0.eng.d
1.2.23. 008   ......s1997....dcu..........f000.0.eng.d
1.2.24. 008   ......s1997....moua..........001.0.eng.d
1.2.25. 008   ......s1997....akua..........000.0.eng.d
```

1.4. Tagging Exercise Answers

Main entries

1.4.1.	100 1	≠a Jones, Jessie.
1.4.2.	100 1	≠a Garcia Lorca, Jose.
1.4.3.	110 1	≠a Louisiana. ≠b Legislature. ≠b Senate.
1.4.4.	110 2	≠a Louisiana Academy of Sciences.
1.4.5.	110 2	≠a Kisatchie National Forest.
1.4.6.	100 1	≠a Petrovsky, Alexandrovitch, ≠d 1902-
1.4.7.	100 1	≠a Spate, Gaspar J. ≠q (Gaspar Julius), ≠d 1881-1956.
1.4.8.	100 0	≠a Paul, ≠c of Byzantium.
1.4.9.	110 2	≠a Balfa Brothers (Musical group)
1.4.10.	110 1	≠a Shreveport (La.). ≠b Police Jury. ≠b Library Committee.
1.4.11.	110 2	≠a Regional Planning Council for Southwest Louisiana.
1.4.12.	100 1	≠a Nixon, Richard M.
1.4.13.	100 1	≠a Pennyfeather, John, ≠c Sir, ≠d 1770-1820.
1.4.14.	111 2	≠a Monroe Bowling Tournament ≠d (1983 : ≠c Monroe, La.)

Title statements

1.4.15.	245 10	≠a Guide to writing tree ordinances / ≠c prepared by Buck Abbey.
1.4.16.	245 10	≠a "Blood will tell!" / ≠c Joseph Bosco.
1.4.17.	245 00	≠a Reflections in time / ≠c Elizabeth Crane, editor.
1.4.18.	245 14	≠a The vampire companion / ≠c Katherine Ramsland.
1.4.19.	245 15	≠a The "Gimme something mister" guide to Mardi Gras / ≠c by Arthur Hardy.
1.4.20.	245 10	≠a Guide de Nouvelle Orleans ≠h [sound recording] = ≠b Guide to New Orleans / ≠c by John Candy.
1.4.21.	245 10	≠a Tell me more ; or, The Hollywood gossip book / ≠c by Nancy Davis Reagan.
1.4.22.	245 14	≠a The stumpin' grounds : ≠b a memoir of New Orleans' Ninth Ward / ≠c by Russell E. Wyman.
1.4.23.	245 10	≠a ... So I told him no : ≠b the trail to the Vice-Presidency / ≠c by Al Gore.
1.4.24.	245 10	≠a Fort Claiborne / ≠c prepared by Cecil Atkinson.
1.4.25.	245 00	≠a Hobnails and helmets / ≠c William H. Burkhart ... [et al.]
1.4.26.	245 14	≠a The analysis of the law / ≠c Sir Matthew Hale.
1.4.27.	245 00	≠a BBC adult literacy handbook / ≠c edited by Chris Longley.

Publication, Distribution, etc.

1.4.28.	260	≠a New York : ≠b Greenwillow Press, ≠c [1949].
1.4.29.	260	≠a Washington D.C. : ≠b U.S. Department of Agriculture : [for sale by the U.S. G.P.O.], ≠c 1964.
1.4.30.	260	≠a London : ≠b Haynes ; ≠a Brookstone, Ct. : ≠b Auto Museum, ≠c c1997.
1.4.31.	260	≠a [Bohemia, La.?] : ≠b L.B. Oppenheimer, ≠c 1957.
1.4.32.	260	≠a [Baton Rouge] : ≠b Louisiana State University Press, ≠c 1985.
1.4.33.	260	≠a Toronto ; New York : ≠b Bantam, ≠c c1952.
1.4.34.	260	≠a [S.l. : ≠b s.n.], ≠c 1935.
1.4.35.	260	≠a Paris : ≠b LeBlanc et cie., ≠c 1935, c1899.
1.4.36.	260	≠a Bayou Manchac, La. : ≠b [s.n., ≠c 19--?]
1.4.37.	260	≠a Alexandria, La. : ≠b Alexandria Museum of Art, ≠c c1977.

Physical Description

1.4.38.	300	≠a 3 v. ; ≠c 30 cm. + ≠e atlas (301 leaves of plates : maps)
1.4.39.	300	≠a 64 p. : ≠b maps ; ≠c 32 cm.
1.4.40.	300	≠a 65 leaves, 102 p., [8] p. of plates : ≠b ill. ; ≠c 16 cm.
1.4.41.	300	≠a xlv, 789 p. : ≠b ill., ports., maps (1 fold.) ; ≠c 13 cm.
1.4.42.	300	≠a 251 p. ; ≠c 22 cm.
1.4.43.	300	≠a 1 videocassette (22 min.) : ≠b sd., col. ; ≠c 1/2 in.
1.4.44.	300	≠a 1 microscope slide : ≠b glass ; ≠c 8 x 3 cm.
1.4.45.	300	≠a 1 game (15 pieces) : ≠b col., cardboard ; ≠c 9 x 12 in.
1.4.46.	300	≠a v. : ≠b ill., maps ; ≠c 28 cm.
1.4.47.	300	≠a 2 film reels (60 min. ea.) : ≠b sd., b&w ; ≠c 16 mm.
1.4.48.	300	≠a ii, 14, vi, 61 p. : ≠b ill., facsims. ; ≠c 16 x 12 cm.
1.4.49.	300	≠a 1 score : ≠b 16 p. of music ; ≠c 28 cm.
1.4.50.	300	≠a 1 v. (various pagings) ; ≠c 26 cm.
1.4.51.	300	≠a 1 sound disc (65 min.) : ≠b digital, stereo. ; ≠c 4 3/4 in.

Series statement

1.4.52.	440 _ 0	≠a Preservation guide
1.4.53.	490 0 _	≠a Fodor guidebook series
1.4.54.	440 _ 0	≠a Nicholls State University. ≠b Center for Traditional Louisiana Boatbuilding. ≠t Wooden boat series
1.4.55.	490 0 _	≠a Report / University of Southwestern Louisiana. Center for Archaeological Studies
1.4.56.	440 _ 0	≠a Water resources series. ≠p North Louisiana subseries.

1.4.57. 490 1 _ ≠a Research / Louisiana State Dept. of Education. Vocational Education Section.

1.4.58. 490 0 _ ≠a State practice series

Notes

1.4.59. 500 ≠a Title from disk label.

1.4.60. 520 ≠a Summary: Biography of Shaquille O'Neal.

1.4.61. 501 ≠a With: Only in your arms / Lisa Kleypas.

1.4.62. 504 ≠a Includes discography (p. 547-569).

1.4.63. 500 ≠a Title supplied by cataloger.

1.4.64. 500 ≠a Reprint. Originally published: Boston : Grey, 1896.

1.4.65. 511 ≠a Cast: Ronald Reagan, Bill Clinton, Richard Nixon.

1.4.66. 505 0 _ ≠a Contents: Hey look me over -- Louisiana hayride -- Cajun two-step -- When the saints go marching in -- Bayou blues -- LSU alma mater.

1.4.67. 502 ≠a Ph.D. (Library Science)--Duke University, 1978.

1.4.68. 500 ≠a Includes index.

1.4.69. 500 ≠a Editor, 1987- : Bobby Ferguson.

Subject Descriptors

1.4.70. 600 1 0 ≠a Nixon, Richard M.

1.4.71. 650 _ 0 ≠a Gardening ≠z Louisiana ≠z New Orleans.

1.4.72. 610 1 0 ≠a Louisiana. ≠b Office of the Lieutenant Governor.

1.4.73. 610 2 0 ≠a State Library of Louisiana. ≠b Technical Services Branch.

1.4.74. 650 _ 0 ≠a Cookery (Oysters)

1.4.75. 610 2 0 ≠a Daughters of the Confederacy. ≠b Louisiana Chapter. ≠b Baton Rouge Post.

1.4.76. 651 _ 0 ≠a Port Allen (La.) ≠x Politics and government.

1.4.77. 651 _0 ≠a Alexandria (La.) ≠x History ≠y Civil War, 1861-1865.

1.4.78. 600 1 0 ≠a Lawrence, Elizabeth, ≠d 1904-1985.

1.4.79. 650 _ 0 ≠a Physically handicapped artists ≠z Louisiana.

1.4.80. 600 3 0 ≠a Ferguson family.

1.4.81. 610 2 0 ≠a Paul M. Hebert Law Center.

1.4.82. 651 _ 0 ≠a Lafourche Parish (La.) ≠x Description and travel.

1.4.83. 610 1 0 ≠a Lafayette Parish (La.). ≠b Office of the Mayor.

1.4.84. 610 2 0 ≠a New Tickfaw Baptist Church (Livingston Parish, La.)

1.4.85. 600 0 0 ≠a Joan, ≠c of Arc, Saint.

1.4.86. 651 _ 0 ≠a Pilottown (La.) ≠x History.

1.4.87. 600 1 0 ≠a Hunter, Bruce, ≠d 1958-

1.4.88. 651 _ 0 ≠a East Feliciana Parish (La.) ≠x Economic aspects.

1.4.89. 650 _ 0 ≠a Hurricanes ≠z Louisiana ≠z Cheniere Caminada.

1.4.90. 611 2 0 ≠a Grand Isle Tarpon Rodeo ≠n (26th : ≠d 1979)

1.4.91. 630 0 0 ≠a Bible. ≠p O.T. ≠p Genesis.

Full records

1.4.92.

110 1 _ ≠a Alabama. ≠b Alcoholic Beverage Control Board.

245 1 0 ≠a Annual beer report / ≠c Alabama Alcoholic Beverage Control Board.

260 ≠a Montgomery, Ala. : ≠b The Board.

300 ≠a v. ; ≠c 28 cm.

310 ≠a Annual

500 ≠a Description based on: October 1, 1977-Sept. 30, 1978.

500 ≠a Title from cover.

500 ≠a Report year ends Sept. 30.

650 _ 0 ≠a Brewing industry ≠z Alabama ≠x Statistics.

1.4.93.

245 0 0 ≠a Marching bands & corps.

246 1 0 ≠a Marching bands and corps.

260 ≠a [Jacksonville, Fla. : ≠b River City Publications], ≠c 1967-

300 ≠a v. : ≠b ill. ; ≠c 28 cm.

310 ≠a Monthly.

362 0 ≠a 1967-

500 ≠a Includes index.

650 _ 0 ≠a Bands (Music)

1.4.94.

100 1 ≠a Milne, A. A. ≠q (Alan Alexander), ≠d 1882-1956.

245 1 4 ≠a The house at Pooh Corner / ≠c by A.A. Milne ; illustrated by Kate Greenaway.

260 ≠a Chicago, Ill. : ≠b Children's Press, ≠c c1983.

300 ≠a 128 p. : ≠b ill. ; ≠c 21 cm.

440 _ 0 ≠a World's greatest classics

700 1 ≠a Greenaway, Kate.

1.4.95.

100 1	≠a Grahame, Kenneth.
245 1 4	≠a The wind in the willows / ≠c by Kenneth Grahame ; illustrated by Robert J. Lee.
260	≠a New York : ≠b Dell, ≠c 1973, c1969.
300	≠a 244 p. : ≠b ill. ; ≠c 19 cm.
500	≠a "A Yearling book."

1.4.96.

100 1	≠a Alford, Gilbert K.
245 1 0	≠a Alford ancestors and descendants : ≠b Jacob and Alvina Alford, the Allfords, and related families / ≠c by Gil and Anna Alford.
250	≠a Rev. ed., with corrections.
260	≠a [S.l.] : ≠b G.K. Alford, ≠c [1986?]
300	≠a x, 279 p. : ≠b ports., facsims., geneal. tables ; ≠c 28 cm.
500	≠a Includes indexes.
600 3 0	≠a Alford family.
651 _ 0	≠a Red River Parish (La.) ≠x Genealogy.
650 _ 0	≠a Marriage records ≠z Louisiana ≠z Red River Parish.
700 1	≠a Alford, Anna.

1.4.97.

100 1	≠a Stratton, Joanna L.
245 1 0	≠a Pioneer women : ≠b voices from the Kansas frontier / ≠c Joanna L. Stratton ; introduced by Arthur M. Schlesinger, Jr.
250	≠a 1st ed.
260	≠a New York : ≠b Simon & Schuster, ≠c c1981.
300	≠a 319 p., [16] leaves of plates : ≠b ill. ; ≠c 24 cm.
504	≠a Includes bibliographical references (p. [305]-307) and index.
650 _ 0	≠a Women ≠z Kansas ≠x History.
650 _ 0	≠a Pioneers ≠z Kansas ≠x History.

1.4.98.

245 0 4	≠a The Bishop's bounty / ≠c compiled by The Bishop's Bounty Cookbook Committee, Saint Mary's Parents' Group, Inc., Saint Mary's Training School for Retarded Children.
260	≠a Alexandria, La. : ≠b Saint Mary's Parents' Group, ≠c c1987.
300	≠a 318 p. : ≠b ill. ; ≠c 24 cm.

500	≠a Includes index.
650 _ 0	≠a Cookery, American ≠x Louisiana style.
710 2	≠a Saint Mary's Training School for Retarded Children (Alexandria, La.). ≠b Saint Mary's Parents' Group.

1.4.99.

245 0 4	≠a Les blues de Balfa ≠h [videorecording] : ≠b with Cajun visits/Visites Cajun.
260	≠a San Francisco, Calif. : ≠b Aginsky Productions, ≠c c1983, c1981.
300	≠a 1 videocassette (20, 16 min.) : ≠b sd., col. ; ≠c ½ in.
538	≠a VHS format.
520	≠a Summary: The story of the Balfa Brothers, and a visit to Cajun country.
650 _ 0	≠a Cajuns ≠z Louisiana.
600 1 0	≠a Balfa, Dewey.
610 2 0	≠a Balfa Brothers (Musical group)
740 0 2	≠a Cajun visits.
740 0 2	≠a Visites Cajun.

1.4.100.

100 1	≠a Darensbourg, Joe, ≠d 1906-1985.
245 1 0	≠a Jazz odyssey : ≠b the autobiography of Joe Darensbourg / ≠c as told to Peter Vacher.
246 1 0	≠a Telling it like it is.
260	≠a Baton Rouge : ≠b Louisiana State University Press, ≠c 1988, c1987.
300	≠a vi, 231 p., [32] p. of plates : ≠b ports. ; ≠c 25 cm.
504	≠a Includes bibliographical references (p. [197]-207) and index.
500	≠a Published in England under the title: Telling it like it is.
600 1 0	≠a Darensbourg, Joe, ≠d 1906-1985.
650 _ 0	≠a Jazz musicians ≠z Louisiana ≠z New Orleans.
700 1	≠a Vacher, Peter, ≠d 1937-

1.4.101.

100 1	≠a Kilbourne, Richard Holcomb.
245 1 2	≠a A history of the Louisiana Civil Code : ≠b the formative years, 1803-1839 / ≠c Richard Holcomb Kilbourne, Jr.
260	≠a [Baton Rouge] : ≠b Publications Institute, Paul M. Hebert Law Center, Louisiana State University, ≠c c1987.

300	≠a xv, 268 p. ; ≠c 24 cm.
500	≠a "Prepared under the auspices of the Center of Civil Law Studies".--t.p.
504	≠a Includes bibliographical references and index.
650 _ 0	≠a Civil law ≠z Louisiana ≠x History.
650 _ 0	≠a Civil law ≠z Louisiana ≠x Codification ≠x History.
710 2	≠a Paul M. Hebert Law Center.

1.5. Series Exercise Answers

1.5.1.	490 0_	≠a Rechtschistorisch Instituut ; ≠v serie 1
1.5.2.	440 _0	≠a SUNY series in new directions in crime and justice studies
1.5.3.	800 1_	≠a Bentham, Jeremy, ≠d 1748-1832. ≠t Defense of usury
	440 _0	≠a Defense of usury
1.5.4.	440 _0	≠a AAR studies in religion
	490 1_	≠a AAR studies in religion / American Academy of Religion
	810 2_	≠a American Academy of Religion. ≠t AAR studies in religion
1.5.5.	440 _0	≠a Inspector Henry Tibbett mystery
1.5.6.	400 10	≠a Lane, Roger. ≠t History of crime and criminal justice series
1.5.7.	440 _0	≠a Prehistoric animals ; ≠v vol. 3
1.5.8.	490 1_	≠a Medical problems ; pt. 2, Blood problems / Suellen Probity
	800 1_	≠a Probity, Suellen. ≠t Medical problems. ≠n pt. 2, ≠p Blood problems
1.5.9.	490 0_	≠a Contemporary questions / J. Wesley Smith
1.5.10.	490 1_	≠a VGM career books (VGM Career Horizons)
	830 1_	≠a VGM career books
1.5.11.	440 _0	≠a Smithsonian guides
1.5.12.	490 1_	≠a A Macmillan reference book
	830 _0	≠a Macmillan reference books
1.5.13.	490 0_	≠a Betterway woodworking plans series
	490 1_	≠a Woodworking plans series
	830 _0	≠a Betterway woodworking plans series
1.5.14.	440 _4	≠a The Smithsonian guide to historic America ; ≠v vol. 1
1.5.15.	490 1_	≠a Civil service test tutor (Arco Publishing House)
	830 _0	≠a Civil service test tutor
1.5.16.	440 _0	≠a Chilton's total car care
	490 0_	≠a Total car care

1.5.17.	440 _0	≠a Mitchell manuals for the automotive professional
1.5.18.	440 _0	≠a D.A.E. research report
	490 0_	≠a Research report / Louisiana State Agricultural Center, Louisiana Agricultural Experiment Station, Dept. of Agricultural Economics and Agribusiness
1.5.19.	490 1_	≠a Information series / Louisiana State University Agricultural Center, Louisiana Agricultural Experiment Station, Department of Agricultural Economics and Agribusiness
	830 _0	≠a A.E.A. information series
1.5.20.	490 1_	≠a Guitar tunes for country players / Willie Sewell
	800 1_	≠a Sewell, Willie. ≠t Guitar tunes for country players

1.6. Error Identification Exercise Answers

1.6.1.	100 1	≠a Smith, John, ≠ⓩ 1956- .	d
1.6.2.	(110)2	≠a Garcia Williams, John.	100
1.6.3.	110②	≠a Port Allen (La.). ≠b Parish Council.	1
1.6.4.	100②	≠a Minnie Pearl, ≠d 1921-1967.	0
1.6.5.	111①	≠a Basketball championship ≠d (1995)	2
1.6.6.	(240)1 2	≠a A dictionary of dogs.	245
1.6.7.	245 1⓪	≠a The horse runs / ≠c John Equus.	4
1.6.8.	245 1④	≠a Everybody wins! / ≠c Polly Tishan.	0
1.6.9.	246 1④	≠a You @#$%^&*!!!	0
1.6.10.	245 1 2	≠a A man for all seasons /≠ⓑ Jim Doe.	c
1.6.11.	260	≠a New York : ≠b○c1996.	Viking ; ≠c
1.6.12.	260	≠a○Libraries Unlimited, ≠c c1996.	Englewood, Co. : ≠b
1.6.13.	260	≠a Converse, La. : ≠b Lewis Pub., ≠ⓓc1990.	c
1.6.14.	260⓪	≠a Gem, KS : ≠b J.W. Pub. Co., ≠c c1982.	*[blank]*
1.6.15.	300	≠a 123 p. : ≠ⓒ ill. ; ≠c 22 cm.	b
1.6.16.	300	≠a 54 p. ; ≠ⓑ 25 cm.	c
1.6.17.	300	≠ⓑ 2 v. ; ≠c 26 cm.	a
1.6.18.	300	≠a 145 p. : ≠b maps, ill. ; ≠c (1965-)	*[space]* cm.
1.6.19.	(301)	≠a 13 v. : ≠b ill. ; ≠c 25 cm.	300
1.6.20.	600②0	≠a Ferguson, A. S. ≠q (Anna S.)	1
1.6.21.	650(1 0)	≠a Basketball ≠x History.	_ 0
1.6.22.	(650)0	≠a Indiana ≠x Description and travel.	651

1.6.23.	610 2 0	≠a Art for New Artists Conference.	611
1.6.24.	651 0	≠x Alaska ≠x Politics and government.	a
1.6.25.	650 0	≠a Automobiles ≠y Maintenance and repair.	x
1.6.26.	651 2 0	≠a Bible ≠x Commentaries.	630 00
1.6.27.	611 2 0	≠a International Film Festival ≠p (1996)	d
1.6.28.	600 2 0	≠a Annette (Actress)	00
1.6.29.	653 0	≠a Detective and mystery stories.	655 _7
1.6.30.	650 0	≠y Twentieth century.	a
1.6.31.	651 2 0	≠a Chicago Bulls.	610
1.6.32.	630 0 0	≠t Bible. ≠p O.T. ≠p Psalms ≠x Commentaries.	a

Multiple Errors Exercise Answers

q
1.6.33. 100 1 ≠a Smith-Rosen, G. N. ≠p (Guy Ngo)

1 ; b
1.6.34. 110 2 ≠a Many (La.). ≠c Mayor.

a d
1.6.35. 100 1 ≠q Smith, John Bob, ≠y 1901-1946.

2)
1.6.36. 111 1 ≠a Golf days ≠n (10th : ≠d 1990 ; ≠c Many (La.)

1 b
1.6.37. 110 2 ≠a Louisiana. ≠a Office of Marine Fisheries.

1
1.6.38. 245 0 0 ≠a The tale of two kitties / ≠c by Mama Cat.

1 g
1.6.39. 245 0 0 ≠b Dogs : ≠b a long tale / ≠c compiled by John Reeder.

5 4 c
1.6.40. 24 0 0 ≠a The sound and the fury / ≠b Ralph Nader.

4
1.6.41. 245 1 5 ≠a Les miserables / ≠c illustrated by Pablo Picasso.

5 / c
1.6.42. 24 6 14 ≠a The soccer defeat : ≠b by the Boston Jets.

[blank] *[publisher]* c *[blank]*
1.6.43. 260 0 ≠a New York : ≠b Milwaukee, ≠b c1946, ≠c 1982.

0 , La. *[blank]* b c
1.6.44. 26 1 ≠a Many ; ≠a Shreveport ; ≠a Reeves, ≠a c1996.

≠a c 1963
1.6.45. 260 New York : ≠b Viking, ≠b 1693.

New York Viking Press *[date]*
1.6.46. 260 ≠a (Viking Press) : ≠b (New York) ; ≠c (28 cm.)

a b c
1.6.47. 260 ≠ⓧ Baton Rouge : ≠ⓐ Ferguson Frolics, ≠ⓨ c1992.

[blank] : b c
1.6.48. 300 ① ≠a 2 v.(;) ≠ⓐ ill., maps, ports ; ≠ⓑ 8 in.

0 1 v. (various pagings) c
1.6.49. 30① ≠a (x, 145, vi, 632, ix, 15 p.) ; ≠ⓑ 22 cm.

c
1.6.50. 300 ≠a 92 p. : ≠b col. ill., facsims. ; ≠ⓩ 28 x 22 cm.

≠a (p.) : ≠b (ill.?) ; ≠c (size)
1.6.51. 300 (≠a : ≠b)

≠a [S.l. : ≠b s.n., ≠c 1995].
1.6.52. 300 (≠a [S.l.] : ≠b [s.n.], ≠c [1995].)

q d
1.6.53. 600 10 ≠a Smith, J. B. ≠ⓧ (John Bob), ≠ⓨ 1952-

2
1.6.54. 610 ①0 ≠a Louisiana Rodeo Association.

2 ≠a (c
1.6.55. 611 ①0 ≠a Lutcher Rodeo Days ((≠a) 1st : ≠d 1996 ; ≠ⓑ Lutcher, La.)

1
1.6.56. 65⓪ 0 ≠a Sabine Parish (La.)

x and travel.
1.6.57. 651 0 ≠a Louisiana ≠ⓩ Description (.)

x ≠y
1.6.58. 650 0 ≠a Cherokee Indians ≠ⓨ History (,) 18th century.

5 *[blank]* *[blank]*
1.6.59. 6⓪0 ⓪0 ≠a Jeremiah (≠x) (Fictitious character) ≠x Fiction.

5 *[blank]* (Fictitious character)
1.6.60. 6⓪0 ⓪0 ≠a F'lar ,(≠q of Pern, ≠c Dragonrider.)

610 10 .
1.6.61. (651 0) ≠a Louisiana ◯ ≠b Office of Tourism.

3 .
1.6.62. 600 ①0 ≠a Jones family(≠x Genealogy.)

1 .
1.6.63. 600 ②0 ≠a Smith, Robbie(, ≠x Biography.)

1 (La.) .
1.6.64. 610 ②0 ≠a Baton Rouge(, Lousiana) (:) ≠b Mayor.

a .≠p .≠p
1.6.65. 630 00 ≠(t) Bible(,) N.T. (,) Matthew.

1.6.66. (10 errors)

d
100 1 ≠a Smith, James D., ≠(c) 1956-

0
245 1(4) ≠a Dogs of the world / ≠c by Jim Smith, Jr.

1st ed.
250 ≠a (**First edition.**)

New York
260 ≠a (**N.Y.**) : ≠b Viking Press, ≠c c1995.

: b ;
300 ≠a ix, 256 p. (;) ≠(c) col. ill.(,) ≠c c1995.

≠a ***[blank]***
440 0 (**≠t**) Animals of the world(.)

500 ≠a Includes Index.

x
650 0 ≠a Dogs ≠(z) Encyclopedias.

1.6.67. (11 errors)

1 b
110 (2) ≠a Louisiana. ≠(p) State Records Office.

5 /
24(0) 10 ≠a Registry of state lands (:) ≠c Louisiana State Records Office.

250 ≠a 1996 ed.

b c
260 ≠a Baton Rouge : ≠(c) The Office, ≠(b) 1996.

c
300 ≠a 1 v. (various pagings) ; ≠(b) 28 cm.

500 ≠a Cover title.

0 a
50(4) ≠(c) Includes index.

651 0 ≠a Louisiana ≠x Registers.

z
650 0 ≠a Land use ≠(x) Louisiana.

Delete this whole line--it is a duplicate of the 110 field.
(**710 2 ≠a Louisiana. ≠b State Records Office.**)

1.6.68. (16 errors)

0 a
1(1)0 1 ≠(c) Robb, Randall R.

1 /
245 (0)4 ≠a The archer looses an arrow (:) ≠c by Randall R. Robb and Sturgis S. Stubbs.

246 30 ≠a Into the air.

≠a 1
250 (≠1) st ed.

300 ≠a 540 p. ; ≠c 18 cm.

a
440 0 ≠(t) Soldiery

Add this line to explain the added title field.

(500 ≠a Formerly published as: Into the air.)

5 7 ≠2 gsafd
65(0) (0) ≠a Detective and mystery stories.( )

5 7 a Historical ≠2 gsafd
65(1) (0) ≠(b) (Medieval) fiction. ( )

1
700 (2) ≠a Stubbs, Sturgis S.

1.6.69. (19 errors)

1 . ≠b
110 (2) ≠a Wisconsin( ) Library of the Arts.

0 a b
245 1(4) ≠(t) Inventory control at the Library of the Arts : ≠(c) a manual

c
of procedures / ≠(b) by the staff of the Wisconsin Library of the Arts.

[blanks] leaves c 28 cm.
300 (00) ≠a 25 (l.) : ≠b ill. ; ≠(b) (11.5 in.)

504 **Includes bibliographical references and index**
(500 00) ≠a (Includes index and bibliography).

1 1
6(5)0 (0)0 ≠a Wisconsin. ≠b Library of the Arts ≠x Handbooks, manuals, etc.

[blank] *[blank]*
650 (0)0 ≠a Art(.) ≠x Preservation.

[blank] a
650 (1)0 ≠(x) Books ≠x Repair.

Delete this entire field. It is a duplicate of the 110 field.

(710 2 ≠a Wisconsin Library of the Arts.)

1.6.70. (7 errors)

```
 1  1                     .
1⓪0 ②              ≠a Michigan◯≠b Dept. of Highways.

245 10             ≠a Michigan highways.

                     a
300                ≠ⓥ v. : ≠b ill., maps ; ≠c 28 cm.

321                ≠a Annual

362 0              ≠a Vol. 1, no. 1- (September 1852)-

                     a
500                ≠ⓠ Title from cover.

  1                  a
65⓪ 0              ≠ⓧ Michigan ≠x Periodicals.
```

1.6.71. (11 errors)

```
    1                a                        b
110 ②              ≠ⓧ Philadelphia (Pa.). ≠ⓟ City Council.

  5   4
24⑥ 1⓪             ≠a The early history of Philadelphia : ≠b from its founding to 1900.

                     [Asterisk]
250                ≠a (*) ed.

                                      p.
300                ≠a xix, 312 p., [16] (pages) of plates : ≠b ill., maps, ports. ; ≠c 28 cm.

  1                  a             (Pa.)             .
65⓪ 0              ≠ⓑ Philadelphia(, Pennsylvania) ≠x History(and description.)
```

1.6.72. (15 errors)

```
100 1                a                     (Albert George)
(245 1 0)          ≠ⓠ Milne, A. G. ≠q (Albert George).

      4                             Spain              /
245 1⓪             ≠a The plane in (Spane) mainly falls (;) ≠c A.G. Milne.

  0                          ed.
25①                ≠a 16th (edition)

                       New York : ≠b                      c
260                ≠a (              ) Little House Press, ≠ⓓ c1992.
```

b cm.
300 ≠a xxxviii, 24 pages : ≠(c) ill., maps ; ≠c (c1992).

0 0 z
65(1) (1) ≠a Aircraft ≠(x) Spain.

1.6.73. (16 errors)

0 0
1(1)0 (0) ≠a Gargantua, Draconus.

5 10 c
24(0) ≠a My life as the Black Dragon / ≠(b) Draconus Gargantua.

6 Publisher, ≠c
2(5)0 ≠a Munich, Germany : ≠b ( ) c1994.

a ill. geneal. ≠c
300 ≠(A) 365 p. ; ≠b (illus.), (gen.) tables ; ( )27 cm.

0 ≠ [ ]
490(0) (/) a My life series (.)

0 0 Draconus
6(5)0 (0) ≠a Gargantua, (Draconius).

1.6.74. (18 errors)

[blank]
100 1(0) ≠a Chan, Lois Mai.

5 0 a classification :
24(4) 1(4) ≠(b) Dewey decimal (classfication) (/) ≠b a practical guide /

≠ .
(◆)c Lois Mai Chan ... et. al.] ( )

0 rev.
25(5) ≠a 2nd ed. (Revised)

0 , N.Y.
26(6) ≠a Albany( ): ≠b Forest Press, ≠c 1996.

a ; c 22 cm.
300 ≠(A) 322 p.( ) ≠(b) (8 1/2 in.)

4 Includes
50(0) ≠a (Contains) bibliographical references and index.

650 0 ≠a Classification, Dewey decimal.

2.1. *AACR2R* Areas Exercise Answers

2.1.1. .1
2.1.2. .4
2.1.3. .7
2.1.4. .8
2.1.5. .0
2.1.6. .2
2.1.7. .9
2.1.8. .5
2.1.9. .3
2.1.10. .6
2.1.11. .10
2.1.12. .11
2.1.13. Edition area, General rules
2.1.14. Cartographic materials, Publication, distribution area
2.1.15. Computer files, Title and statement of responsibility area
2.1.16. Three-dimensional artefacts and realia, General rules
2.1.17. Sound recordings, Material specific details area
2.1.18. Graphic materials, Physical description area
2.1.19. Books, pamphlets and printed sheets, Series area
2.1.20. Music, Standard number and terms of availability area
2.1.21. Manuscripts, Note area
2.1.22. Microforms, Physical description area

2.2. *AACR2R* General Exercise Answers

2.2.1. Jean Weihs.
2.2.2. Michael Gorman and Paul W. Winkler.
2.2.3. .0B [zero B]
2.2.4. .0D [zero D]
2.2.5. .0C [zero C]
2.2.6. Transcribe the inaccuracy or misspelling as it appears in the item. Follow that with either [sic] or i.e., *[correction]*. You can also supply a missing letter or letters in square brackets.
2.2.7. .0F [zero F]
2.2.8. .0H [zero H]

2.2.9. .0B [zero B]

2.2.10. No. Rule 25.1A.

2.2.11. Roman script. Rule 25.2D1.

2.2.12. 25.2C

2.2.13. No. *AACR2R* contains the rules for descriptive cataloging, not subject cataloging. The only rules governing subjects are those in Part II, which tell you how to formulate names.

2.2.14. 1.1C.

2.2.15. No.

2.2.16. The *Chicago Manual of Style* is the authority. Rule 0.11 [zero.11].

2.2.17. No. The examples illuminate the provisions of the rule to which they are attached only. They are illustrative and not prescriptive.

2.2.18. The *Library of Congress Rule Interpretations (LCRI)*.

2.2.19. Both. *AACR2R* gives rules for the description of materials being cataloged, not how they are input into a computer or typed on a catalog card.

2.2.20. It means that a statement to which it applies must be a format statement found in one of the prescribed sources of information in areas 1 and 2. Rule 0.8 gives this definition.

2.2.21. No.

2.2.22. Not if they are designated as **optional**. You may do so to avoid conflicts in the future.

2.2.23. No, they don't. If no specific rule applies, use the general rule from Chapter 1.

2.2.24. No, never.

2.2.25. Yes. Rule 21.1B1.

2.3. *AACR2R*, Part I Exercise Answers

2.3.1. The title page, or if there is no title page, the source from within the publication that is used for it.

2.3.2. The part of the item supplying the most complete information. It may be the cover, half title page, caption, colophon, running title, or other part.

2.3.3. Sources of information other than the chief source. Used for information found in various areas of the bibliographical record.

2.3.4. No. You are told to use the general statement given in Rule 1.0F.

2.3.5. Preceding the information.

2.3.6. For an oriental, non-roman script publication, if the colophon contains full bibliographic information.

2.3.7. Any source.

2.3.8. 2.0D, 2.0E, 2.0F, 2.0G, 2.0H

2.4. Personal Authors (Chapter 22) Exercise Answers

2.4.1. *AACR2R* rule: 22.2B1
Read, Miss.

2.4.2. *AACR2R* rule: 22.11A
Grandfather Weeks.

2.4.3. *AACR2R* rule: 22.11B
Belle, Cousin.

2.4.4. *AACR2R* rule: 22.10A
D. de F.

2.4.5. *AACR2R* rule: 22.8A1
Pliny, the Elder.

2.4.6. *AACR2R* rule: 22.13B
Augustine, Saint, Bishop of Hippo.

2.4.7. *AACR2R* rule: 22.5C3
Day-Lewis, Cecil.

2.4.8. *AACR2R* rule: 22.16A3
Philip, Prince, consort of Elizabeth II, Queen of the United Kingdom.

2.4.9. *AACR2R* rule: 22.3C1
Alexander, the Great.

2.4.10. *AACR2R* rule: 22.12B1
Christie, Agatha.

2.4.11. *AACR2R* rule: 22.6A1
Byron, George Gordon Byron, Baron.

2.4.12. *AACR2R* rule: 22.9A
Cicero, Marcus Tullius.

2.4.13. *AACR2R* rule: 22.5C4
Tall Chief, Maria.

2.4.14. *AACR2R* rule: 22.12B1
Brown, Sir George.

2.4.15. *AACR2R* rule: 22.16B1
Leo XIII, Pope.

2.4.16. *AACR2R* rule: 22.18A
Wells, H. G. (Herbert George)

2.4.17. *AACR2R* rule: 22.11A
Buckskin Bill.

2.4.18. *AACR2R* rule: 22.2B1
Allen, Woody.

2.4.19. *AACR2R* rule: 22.2B3
Michaels, Barbara.

2.4.20. *AACR2R* rule: 22.1B
H. D.

2.4.21. *AACR2R* rule: 22.16A2
Suleiman I, Sultan of the Turks

2.4.22. *AACR2R* rule: 22.5F1
Hohenzollern, Franz, Joseph, Fürst von.

2.4.23. *AACR2R* rule: 22.5E1
MacDonald, Frank.

2.4.24. *AACR2R* rule: 22.15A
Seuss, Dr.

2.4.25. *AACR2R* rule: 22.19B1
Smith, John, captain.

2.5. Corporate Bodies (Chapter 24), Exercise Set 1 Answers

2.5.1. Alabama. Commission on Certification of Social Workers.

2.5.2. First Presbyterian Church (Boise, Idaho)

2.5.3. Montana.

2.5.4. Governor's Conference on Mental Disabilities (3rd : 1957 : Ames, Iowa)

2.5.5. University of Mississippi. Coastal Resources Section.

2.5.6. Catholic Church. Pope (1878-1903 : Leo XIII)

2.5.7. Republican Party (La.). State Committee.

2.5.8. West Baton Rouge Genealogical Society.

2.5.9. Freemasons. Grand Lodge of Lafayette.

2.5.10. United States. Congress. House of Representatives. Committee on Public Health. Subcommittee on the Federal-Aid Adult Daycare Program.

2.5.11. Nebraska. Supreme Court.

2.5.12. Maine Library Association. Technical Services Interest Group.

2.5.13. Kidd (Ship)

2.5.14. Architectural Students Forum (University of New Orleans)

2.5.15. Mississippi. Pearl River Administration.

2.5.16. Jesuits.

2.5.17. Episcopal Church. Diocese of Western Louisiana.

2.5.18. University of Southwestern Louisiana. Center for Louisiana Studies.

2.5.19. KEEL (Radio station : Shreveport, La.)

2.5.20. Lake Providence (La.). Assessor.

2.5.21. Presbyterian Church (U.S.). National Council.

2.5.22. Monitor (Ship)

2.5.23. Holy Jesus Church (Brooklyn, N.Y. : Baptist)

2.5.24. United States. Congress. House of Representatives.

2.5.25. United States. Army. Infantry Division, 16th.

2.5.26. United States. Naval Air Corps.

2.5.27. Louisiana. Constitutional Convention (1989).

2.5.28. Utah. Department of Revenue.

2.5.29. Rice Festival (5th : Cameron, La.)

2.5.30. Red River Compact Administration.

2.5.31. Cheniere Caminada Delta Management Program.

2.5.32. Chile. Embassy (U.S.)

2.5.33. United States. President (1993- : Clinton)

2.5.34. Kaw Valley Film & Video.

Corporate Bodies (Chapter 24), Exercise Set 2 Answers

2.5.35. *AACR2R* rule 24.20C1
Port Allen (La.). Mayor.

2.5.36. *AACR2R* rule 24.11
WJBO (Radio station : Baton Rouge, La.)

2.5.37. *AACR2R* rule 24.4C1
Terrebonne Genealogical Society.

2.5.38. *AACR2R* rule 24.5C4
Louisiana (Ship)

2.5.39. *AACR2R* rule 24.13
Louisiana State University (Baton Rouge, La.). Center for Wetland Resources.

2.5.40. *AACR2R* rule 24.13
Catholic Church. Pope (1978- : John Paul II)

2.5.41. *AACR2R* rule 24.4C2
Republican Party (La.)

2.5.42. *AACR2R* rule 24.16A
Democratic Party (La.). State Committee.

2.5.43. *AACR2R* rule 24.2D
AFL-CIO.

2.5.44. *AACR2R* rule 24.7B
Governor's Conference on Physical Disabilities (2nd : 1978 : New Orleans, La.)

2.5.45. *AACR2R* rule 24.21C
United States. Congress. House of Representatives. Committee on Public Works. Special Subcommittee on the Federal-Aid Highway Program.

2.5.46. *AACR2R* rule 24.18
Mississippi. Environmental Protection Agency.

2.5.47. *AACR2R* rule 24.9A
Freemasons. Grand Lodge of Baton Rouge.

2.5.48. *AACR2R* rule 24.12
Paul M. Hebert Law Center.

2.5.49. *AACR2R* rule 24.4C7
Tiger Tales Club (University of New Orleans)

2.5.50. *AACR2R* rule 24.27C2
Catholic Church. Louisiana Diocese.

2.5.51. *AACR2R* rule 24.3D1
Poor Clares.

2.5.52. *AACR2R* rule 24.23A
Louisiana. Supreme Court.

2.5.53. *AACR2R* rule 24.20B
United States. President (1961-1963 : Kennedy)

2.5.54. *AACR2R* rule 24.10B
First Baptist Church (Big Wood, La.)

2.5.55. *AACR2R* rule 24.19
Louisiana. Bureau of Environmental Health.

2.5.56. *AACR2R* rule 24.24A1
United States. Army Air Corps.

2.5.57. *AACR2R* rule 24.4B
F4 Phantom (Jet plane)

2.5.58. *AACR2R* rule 24.27A1
Episcopal Church (U.S.). National Council.

2.5.59. *AACR2R* rule 24.21A
United States. Congress. Senate.

2.5.60. *AACR2R* rule 24.10
All Saints Church (Manhattan, N.Y. : Catholic)

2.5.61. *AACR2R* rule 24.22B
Louisiana. Constitutional Convention (1973).

2.5.62. *AACR2R* rule 24.24A1
United States. Army. Infantry Division, 25th.

2.5.63. *AACR2R* rule 24.8
Shrimp Festival (3rd : Houma, La.)

2.5.64. *AACR2R* rule 24.18
Louisiana. Department of Culture, Recreation and Tourism.

2.5.65. *AACR2R* rule 24.15A
Sabine River Compact Administration.

2.5.66. *AACR2R* rule 24.18
Mongolia. Embassy (Great Britain)

2.5.67. *AACR2R* rule 24.17
Kisatchie-Delta Regional Management Program.

2.5.68. *AACR2R* rule 24.5C1
Coronet Film and Video.

2.6. Geographic Names, Exercise Set 1 Answers

2.6.1. Paris (France)

2.6.2. Broadmoor (Shreveport, La.)

2.6.3. Beijing (China)

2.6.4. Helsinki (Finland)

2.6.5. Ontario

2.6.6. Fort Erie (Ontario)

2.6.7. York (England)

2.6.8. Ulaanbaatar, Mongolia

2.6.9. Linwood (Bartow County, Ga.)

2.6.10. Linwood (Walker County, Ga.)

2.6.11. Kansas City (Mo.)

Geographic Names, Exercise Set 2 Answers

2.6.12. *AACR2R* rule: 23.4C2
Yellow Creek (Sask.)

2.6.13. *AACR2R* rule: 23.4E
Bonn (Germany)

2.6.14. *AACR2R* rule: 23.5A
Pôrto Mendes (Brazil)

2.6.15. *AACR2R* rule: 23.4D2
Strathaven (Scotland)

2.6.16. *AACR2R* rule: 23.4C1
Queensland

2.6.17. *AACR2R* rule: 23.2B1
Beijing (China)

2.6.18. *AACR2R* rule: 23.4C2
Alice Springs (N.T.)

2.6.19. *AACR2R* rule: 23.4E
Lhasa (Tibet)

2.6.20. *AACR2R* rule: 23.5A
Nuevo Laredo (Mexico)

2.6.21. *AACR2R* rule: 23.4D2
Bushmills (Northern Ireland)

2.6.22. *AACR2R* rule: 23.4C1
Virgin Islands of the United States.

2.6.23. *AACR2R* rule: 23.2B1
Puerta Vallarta (Mexico)

2.6.24. *AACR2R* rule: 23.4C2
Omaha (Neb.)

2.6.25. *AACR2R* rule: 23.4E
Kathmandu (Nepal)

2.6.26. *AACR2R* rule: 23.4D2
Llanelly (Wales)

2.6.27. *AACR2R* rule: 23.5A
Ciudad Hidalgo (Mexico)

2.6.28. *AACR2R* rule: 23.4C1
Yukon

2.7. Choice of Access Points Exercise Answers

2.7.1. The choice of access points, or headings, under which a bibliographic description is entered in a catalog.

2.7.2. Chief source of information, or its substitute.

2.7.3. Compiler, editor, illustrator, translator.

2.7.4. Abbreviated.

2.7.5. No, other designations can be added as instructed in particular rules.

2.7.6. The person chiefly responsible for the creation of the intellectual or artistic content of a work.

2.7.7. 21.1B2

2.7.8. A work emanates from a corporate body if it is issued by that body, or has been caused to be issued by that body, or if it originated with that body.

2.7.9. Treat it as if it doesn't.

2.7.10. Treat it as if no corporate body were involved, and make added entries for prominently named corporate bodies.

2.7.11. Yes. Enter a work under title if (a) the personal author is unknown or diffuse, (b) the work does not emanate from a corporate body, (c) it is produced under editorial direction, (d) it emanates from a corporate body but does not fall into any categories in 21.1B2, or (e) it is accepted as sacred scripture by a religious group.

2.7.12. No.

2.7.13. Consider that the title has changed.

2.7.14. Make a new record.

2.7.15. Make a new record.

2.7.16. Enter it under the corporate heading for the official.

2.7.17. Enter it under the personal name heading, not the corporate name heading.

2.7.18. Enter it under title main entry.

2.7.19. (a) Works produced by two or more persons, (b) works for which different persons have prepared separate contributions, (c) works consisting of an exchange between two or more persons, such as correspondence or debates, (d) works falling into one or more of the categories given in Rule 21.1B2, (e) works consisting of a combination of personal and corporate authors.

2.7.20. When there are more than three authors.

2.7.21. Only the first author is given in the statement of responsibility and only the first is traced as added entry.

2.7.22. The one named first in the chief source of information.

2.7.23. The person named first in the chief source of information.

2.7.24. Each edition is entered under the person entered first on the chief source of information, and the other is traced as an added entry.

2.7.25. Use the pseudonym as the main entry.

2.7.26. Enter it under the heading appropriate to the new work if the modification has substantially changed the nature and content of the original, or if the medium of expression has changed.

2.7.27. Enter it under the heading appropriate to the original.

2.7.28. Enter it under the name of the adapter.

2.7.29. Enter it under the heading appropriate for the original work.

2.7.30. Enter it under the heading appropriate for the original work.

2.7.31. To provide access to bibliographic descriptions in addition to the access provided by the main entry heading.

2.7.32. Persons, corporate bodies, and titles.

2.7.33. Yes.

2.7.34. No.

2.7.35. Not necessarily. There are separate rules dealing with analytical entries, and Rule 21.30M1 states that analytical entries would be made according to the policy of the cataloging agency.

2.7.36. No.

2.8. Uniform Titles Exercise Answers

2.8.1. It is enclosed in square brackets and placed in an indention before the title proper.

2.8.2. Uniform titles appear in 240 fields; titles proper appear in 245 fields. Uniform titles have no initial articles, and titles proper may or may not have initial articles.

2.8.3. No.

2.8.4. Romanize it according to the table for that language adopted by the cataloging agency.

2.8.5. English, French, German, Spanish, Russian.

2.8.6. The language of the edition first received by the library.

2.8.7. Yes, if you use a uniform title at all. If there is only one edition in the library, you may choose not to use a uniform title, but instead put a note about the availability of other editions in other languages.

2.8.8. Use a well-established English title, if there is one. If not, use the Latin title. If there is neither English nor Latin, use the Greek title.

2.8.9. Add in parentheses an appropriate explanatory word, brief phrase, or other designation. [Example: "Charlemagne, Emperor" and "Charlemagne (Play)". In an automated system, the first would be placed in a 100 field, and the second in a 130 field.]

2.8.10. Add parenthetical phrases of versions [for example, (Southern version) or (Northern version)], or add dates.

2.8.11. Put the language of the item being cataloged after a full stop following the uniform title. [Example: Beowulf. French.]

2.8.12. No. Do not add the name of the language to the uniform title.

2.8.13. Add the name of the modern language followed by the name of the early form in parentheses. [Example: English (Middle English)]

2.8.14. Add both languages after the uniform title, the original language named second.

2.8.15. Use the following preference table: English, French, German, Spanish, Russian, other languages in alphabetic order of their names in English.

2.8.16. After the uniform title use "Polyglot".

2.8.17. Use the uniform title for the whole work followed by "Selections".

2.8.18. Use the uniform title "Works".

2.8.19. Use "Selections".

2.8.20. Use one of the following collective titles: Correspondence, Essays, Novels, Plays, Poems, Prose works, Short stories, Speeches.

2.8.21. Use an appropriate specific collective title, such as Posters or Fragments.

2.8.22. Use "Laws, etc.".

2.8.23. Use in this order of preference: (a) the official short title or citation title, (b) an unofficial short title or citation title used in legal literature, (c) the official title of the enactment, or (d) any other official designation such as the number or date.

2.8.24. Add the year of promulgation of the original acts.

2.8.25. Use "Treaties, etc." followed by the name of the other party.

2.8.26. Use "Treaties, etc." by itself.

2.8.27. Use the title by which it is most commonly identified in English-language reference sources dealing with the group to which the scripture belongs.

2.8.28. Use Bible followed by the testament (O.T. or N.T.); the book; the number if it is one of a numbered sequence of the same name such as Corinthians, 1st; the chapter (in roman numerals); and the verse (in Arabic numerals).

2.8.29. Bible, [testament], [special group]. [Example: Bible. N.T. Catholic Epistles.]

2.8.30. Bible. O.T. Apocrypha.

2.8.31. Use the commonly identified title, without initial articles.

2.8.32. Yes, but the first is the main entry and the second is a uniform title added entry.

2.8.33. Use Bible, followed by the language of the item being cataloged, the version, name of the translator, and year.

2.8.34. Put it after the particular part of the Bible included, at the end of the uniform title, just as you would after Bible.

2.8.35. Enter it as a subheading of Talmud or Talmud Yerushalmi, as appropriate.

2.8.36. *Encyclopaedia Judaica.*

2.8.37. Enter them as a subheading of Vedas. If the item is a particular version, add the name of the version in parentheses.

3.2. References Exercise Answers

Personal names, *See From* references

3.2.1. 400 1 Jones, Seymour Rochambaud.
UF Jones, Seymour Rochambaud

3.2.2. 400 1 Faust, Frederick, ≠d 1892-1944.
UF Faust, Frederick, 1892-1944

3.2.3. 400 1 Boynton, Janice Hendricks.
UF Boynton, Janice Hendricks

3.2.4. 400 1 Rice, Katherine.
UF Rice, Katherine

Personal names, *See Also* references

3.2.5. 500 1 Carroll, Lewis, ≠d 1832-1898.
SA Carroll, Lewis, 1832-1898

Corporate names, *See From* references

3.2.6. 410 1 Louisiana. ≠b Dept. of Culture, Recreation and Tourism. ≠b Office of State Library.
UF Louisiana. Dept. of Culture, Recreation and Tourism. Office of State Library

3.2.7. 410 1 Kentucky. ≠b Vocational Education Section.
UF Kentucky. Vocational Education Section

3.2.8. 410 2 BNA.
UF BNA

3.2.9. 410 1 United States. ≠b Interior, Department of the.
UF United States. Interior, Department of the

Corporate names, *See Also* references

3.2.10. 510 2 Louisiana State University (Baton Rouge, La.)
SA Louisiana State University (Baton Rouge, La.)

3.2.11. 510 2 Tulane University. ≠b Newcomb College.
SA Tulane University. Newcomb College

Subject headings, *See From* references

3.2.12. 450 0 Baby sitting.
UF Baby sitting.

3.2.13. 450 0 Homosexuals, Male.
UF Homosexuals, Male

3.2.14. 450 0 Police officers.
UF Police officers

Subject headings, *See Also* references

3.2.15. 550 0 Cookery ≠z Louisiana.
RT Cookery--Louisiana

3.2.16. 550 0 Snakes
NT Snakes

3.2.17. 450 0 Indians of North America
BT Indians of North America

3.2.18. 550 0 Escalators
RT Escalators

Geographical names, *See From* references

3.2.19. 450 0 Kola Peninsula (R.S.F.S.R.)
UF Kola Peninsula (R.S.F.S.R.)

3.2.20. 451 0 St. John the Baptist Parish (La.)
UF St. John the Baptist Parish (La.)

3.2.21. 451 0 Cobb County, Ga.
UF Cobb County, Ga.

3.2.22. 451 0 Commonwealth of Pennsylvania
UF Commonwealth of Pennsylvania

Geographical names, *See Also* references

3.2.23. 551 0 Washington D.C. Regional Area.
SA Washington D.C. Regional Area

3.2.24. 551 0 Vieux Carré (New Orleans, La.) ≠x History.
NT Vieux Carré (New Orleans, La.) ≠x History

3.2.25. 551 0 New York (N.Y.)
BT New York (N.Y.)

3.3 Authority Control, Exercise Set 1 Answers

3.3.1. 100 1 _ ≠a Ferguson, Gary.
670 ≠a His Repairing your power lawnmower, c1992. ≠b t.p. (Gary Ferguson)

3.3.2. 100 1 _ ≠a Lilly, Joyce.
670 ≠a Her Louisiana's highest peak, c1991. ≠b t.p. (Joyce Lilly)

3.3.3. 1 00 1 _ ≠a Jaques, Thomas F.
4 00 1 _ ≠a Jaques, Tom.
5 50 _ 0 ≠a State librarians ≠x Biography.
670 ≠a His Autobiography of a State Librarian, c2001. ≠b t.p. (Thomas F. Jaques ; p. ii, Tom Jaques)

3.3.4. 110 1 _ ≠a Louisiana. ≠b Office of the Governor.
410 1 _ ≠a Louisiana. ≠b Governor, Office of the.
410 1 _ ≠a Louisiana. ≠b Governor's Office.
670 ≠a State of the state report, 1995, 1995. ≠b t.p. (Louisiana Office of the Governor)

3.3.5. 150 _ 0 ≠a Oliver, Gideon (Fictitious character)
450 _ 0 ≠a Gideon Oliver (Fictitious character)
450 _ 0 ≠a Skeleton Detective (Fictitious character)
450 _ 0 ≠a Professor Oliver (Fictitious character)
670 ≠a Elkins, Aaron. The dark place, 1987.

3.3.6. 100 1 _ ≠a Lewis, Marvin W. ≠q (Marvin Wells), ≠d 1964-
400 0 _ ≠a Lewis, Marvin Wells, ≠d 1964-
400 0 _ ≠a Lewis, Trey.
670 ≠a His Indian artifacts of the Gulf Coast, c1998. ≠b t.p. (Marvin Wells Lewis) ; phone call to author (generally known as Trey; born in 1964)

Authority Control, Exercise Set 2 Answers

3.3.7. 008......na.acnndaabn...........a.aaa.....d

3.3.8. 008......na.acnndaabn...........a.aaa.....d

3.3.9. 008......na.acnndaabn...........a.aaa.....d

3.3.10. 008......na.acnndaabn...........a.aaa.....d

3.3.11. 008......na.acnndaabn...........a.aaa.....d

3.3.12. 008......na.acnndaabn...........a.aaa.....d

3.3.13. 008......na.acnndaabn...........a.aaa.....d

3.3.14. 008......na.acnndaabn...........a.aaa.....d

3.3.15. 008......na.acnndaabn..........la.ana.....d

3.3.16. 008......na.acnndaabn...........a.ana.....d

3.3.17. 008......na.acnndaabn...........a.ana.....d

3.3.18. 008......na.acnndaabn...........a.ana.....d

3.3.19. 008......na.acnndaabn..........fa.ana.....d

3.3.20. 008......na.acnndaabn...........a.ana.....d

3.3.21. 008......na.acnndaabn...........a.ana.....d

3.3.22. 008......na.acnndaabn..........sa.ana.....d

3.3.23. 008......ia.acbndbabn...........a.ana.....d

3.3.24. 008......ia.acbndbabn...........a.ana.....d

3.3.25. 008......ia.acbndbabn...........a.ana.....d

3.3.26. 008......ia.acbndbabn...........a.ana.....d

3.3.27. 008......ia.acbndbabn...........a.ana.....d

3.3.28. 008......ia.acbndbabn...........a.ana.....d

3.3.29. 008......ia.acbndbabn...........a.ana.....d

3.3.30. 008......ia.acbndbabn...........a.ana.....d

3.3.31. 008......na.acnabbban...........a.ana.....d

3.3.32. 008......na.acnabbban...........a.ana.....d

3.3.33. 008......na.acnabbban...........a.ana.....d

3.3.34. 008......na.acnabbban...........a.ana.....d

3.3.35. 008......na.acnabbban..........sa.ana.....d

3.3.36. 008......na.acnabbban...........a.ana.....d

3.3.37. 008......na.acnabbban...........a.ana.....d

3.3.38. 008......na.acnabbban...........a.ana.....d

Authority Control, Exercise Set 3 Answers

In these exercises the 040 field is left blank because the answers will vary according to user.

Corporate Names

3.3.39.

008	y y m m d d n a . a c n n d a a b n . . . . a . a a a . . . . . d
040	≠a ____ ≠c ____
110 2 0	≠a Westin Photographic Company.
410 2 0	≠a Westin Films.
410 2 0	≠a Westin Photographs.
670	≠a Its Westin professional moving pictures and stills, c1983. ≠b t.p. (Westin Photographic Company).
670	≠a Smith, William Robert. A Westin history, c1993. ≠b p. ii-iii (established in 1901 as Westin Films ; succeeded by Westin Photographs in 1918; became Westin Photographic Company in 1935. Began publishing in 1952.)

3.3.40.

008	y y m m d d n a . a c n n d a a b n . . . . a . a a a . . . . . d
040	≠a ____ ≠c ____
110 1 0	≠a Louisiana. ≠b Department of Education.
410 1 0	≠a Louisiana. ≠b Education, Department of.
410 1 0	≠a Louisiana. ≠b State Department of Education.
410 1 0	≠a Louisiana. ≠b State Department of Public Education.
670	≠a Louisiana. Bureau of Minority Education. End-of-the-year report for minority education programs, 1984. ≠b t.p. (Louisiana Department of Education); p. 2 (Louisiana State Department of Education).
670	≠a Matt, Katherine. Louisiana history, 1966. ≠b p. 9 (State Department of Public Education).

3.3.41.

008	y y m m d d n a . a c n n d a a b n . . . . a . a a a . . . . . d
040	≠a ____ ≠c ____
110 2 0	≠a Minton-Shropshire Porcelain Company.
510 2 0	≠a Minton-Shropshire Unlimited.
670	≠a Its Pseudo-porcelains, 1895. ≠b (Minton-Shropshire Porcelain Company Limited).
670	≠a William, Teal. The history of the Minton and Shropshire Companies, 1996. (Firm founded in 1832 as Minton-Shropshire Porcelain Company Limited; used "Minton Porcelain Company","Shropshire Porcelain Company" and "M-SP" marks on various manufactures during 1835-1839; renamed Minton-Shropshire Unlimited in 1840).

008 y y m m d d n a . a c n n d a a b n . . . . a . a a a . . . . . d
040 ≠a ____ ≠c ____
110 2 0 ≠a Minton-Shropshire Unlimited.
510 2 0 ≠a Minton-Shropshire Porcelain Company.
670 ≠a William, Teal. The history of the Minton and Shropshire Companies, 1996. (Firm founded in 1832 as Minton-Shropshire Porcelain Company Limited; used "Minton Porcelain Company","Shropshire Porcelain Company" and "M-SP" marks on various manufactures during 1835-1839; renamed Minton-Shropshire Unlimited in 1840).
670 ≠a Its Pseudo-porcelains, 1895. ≠b (Minton-Shropshire Porcelain Company Limited).

3.3.42.

008 y y m m d d n a . a c n n d a a b n . . . . a . a a a . . . . . d
040 ≠a ____ ≠c ____
110 2 0 ≠a National Library of Medicine (U.S.)
410 1 0 ≠a United States. ≠b National Library of Medicine.
410 2 0 ≠a National Institutes of Health (U.S.). ≠b National Library of Medicine.
410 2 0 ≠a NLM
410 2 0 ≠a N.L.M.
670 ≠a U.S. Congress. Senate Committee on the Judiciary. A National Library of Medicine: hearings, 1956. ≠b title (National Library of Medicine)
670 ≠a Centenary of Index Medicus, 1879-1979, 1980. ≠b t.p. (U.S. Department of Health and Human Services, Public Health Service, National Institutes of Health, National Library of Medicine)
670 ≠a Index of NLM serial titles, [1972]- . ≠b title (NLM)

3.3.43.

008 y y m m d d n a . a c n n d a a b n . . . . a . a a a . . . . . d
040 ≠a ____ ≠c ____
110 2 0 ≠a Public Affairs Research Council of Louisiana, inc.
410 2 0 ≠a PAR
410 2 0 ≠a P.A.R.
670 ≠a A PAR report, 1951. ≠b t.p. (Public Affairs Research Council of Louisiana, inc.); title (PAR).
678 ≠a Organized in 1950.

3.3.44.

008 y y m m d d n a . a c n n d a a b n . . . . a . a a a . . . . . d
040 ≠a ____ ≠c ____
110 2 0 ≠a Saint Boudreaux County Public Library.
410 2 0 ≠a St. Boudreaux County Public Library.
670 ≠a Majors, John B. The end of the line, c1975. ≠b t.p. (Saint Boudreaux County Public Library)

3.3.45.

008 y y m m d d n a . a c n n d a a b n . . . . a . a a a . . . . . d

040 ≠a ____ ≠c ____

110 2 0 ≠a Our Lady of the Mountains Undergraduate Library.

410 2 0 ≠a OLM Library.

410 2 0 ≠a Our Lady Undergraduate Library

410 2 0 ≠a University of Guadalupe Libraries. Our Lady of the Mountains Undergraduate Library.

670 ≠a Marsh, Guinevere. University of Guadalupe Libraries, 1993. ≠b p. ii (Our Lady of the Mountains Undergraduate Library, OLM Library).

670 ≠a Sangria, Maria. Holdings in the OLM Library, 1988 ≠b p. iv (OLM Library; Our Lady Undergraduate Library; Our Lady of the Mountains Undergraduate Library)

3.3.46.

008 y y m m d d n a . a c n n d a a b n . . . . a . a a a . . . . . d

040 ≠a ____ ≠c ____

110 2 0 ≠a US3 (Music group)

410 2 0 ≠a US 3 (Music group)

410 2 0 ≠a Us Three (Music group)

670 ≠a Cedar trees of heaven [SR], 1984. ≠b CD label (US3)

670 ≠a Smith, Jim. "US 3 have made it big in the U.S.", Newsweekly, Aug. 15, 1997 (US 3; US3; Us Three)

Geographic Names

3.3.47.

008 y y m m d d n a . a c n n d a a b n . . . . a . a a a . . . . . d

040 ≠a ____ ≠c ____

151 0 ≠a Cape of Good Hope (South Africa : Cape)

451 0 ≠a Good Hope, Cape of (South Africa : Cape)

451 0 ≠a Cape of Storms (South Africa : Cape)

451 0 ≠a Cape Peninsula (South Africa : Cape)

670 ≠a Jarreau, Parkinson. Touring the Cape and the vineyards, 1991. ≠b (Cape of Storms; Cape of Good Hope; Cape Peninsula).

670 ≠a *LCSH*, 20th ed. (1997), v. 1, p. 832.

3.3.48.

008 y y m m d d n a . a c n n d a a b n . . . . a . a a a . . . . . d

040 ≠a ____ ≠c ____

151 0 ≠a Cartagena, Bay of (Colombia)

451 0 ≠a Bay of Cartagena (Colombia)

451 0 ≠a Bahia de Cartagena (Columbia)

550 0 ≠a Bays ≠z Columbia

670 ≠a Willow, Diego. A multisensory picture of Cartagena Bay, Colombia, 1982.
670 ≠a *LCSH*, 20th ed. (1997), v. 2, p. 860 (Cartagena, Bay of (Colombia), UF Bahia de Cartagena (Colombia), Bay of Cartagena (Colombia)); p. 508 (Bays (May Subd Geog)).

008 y y m m d d n a . a c n n d a a b n . . . . a . a a a . . . . . d
040 ≠a ____ ≠c ____
150 0 ≠a Bays ≠z Columbia
551 0 ≠a Cartagena, Bay of (Colombia)
670 ≠a Willow, Diego. A multisensory picture of Cartagena Bay, Colombia, 1982.
670 ≠a *LCSH*, 20th ed. (1997), v. 1, p. 508 (Bays (May Subd Geog)), p. 860 (Cartagena, Bay of (Colombia)).

3.3.49.

008 y y m m d d n a . a c n n d a a b n . . . . a . a a a . . . . . d
040 ≠a ____ ≠c ____
151 0 ≠a Karana (Extinct city)
451 0 ≠a Karana (Ancient city)
451 0 ≠a Tell el-Rimah (Iraq)
550 0 ≠a Extinct cities ≠z Iraq.
670 ≠a Killeen, Sheila. El Souk and Karana, c1976.
670 ≠a *LCSH*, 20th ed. (1997), v. 3, p. 2918 (Karana (Extinct City)) ; UF Karana (Ancient city), Tell el-Rimah; BT Extinct cities--Iraq.

008 y y m m d d n a . a c n n d a a b n . . . . a . a a a . . . . . d
040 ≠a ____ ≠c ____
150 0 ≠a Extinct cities ≠z Iraq.
551 0 ≠a Karana (Extinct city)
670 ≠a Killeen, Sheila. El Souk and Karana, c1976.
670 ≠a *LCSH*, 20th ed. (1997), v. 2, p. 1882 (Extinct cities--Iraq) : v. 3, p. 2918 (Karana (Extinct City)).

3.3.50.

008 y y m m d d n a . a c n n d a a b n . . . . a . a a a . . . . . d
040 ≠a ____ ≠c ____
151 0 ≠a Lake District (England)
451 0 ≠a Lakeland (England)
450 0 ≠a Lakes ≠z England.
670 ≠a Marsh, Inde. Touring the Lake District, 1994.
670 ≠a *LCSH*, 20th ed. (1997), v. 3, p. 3047 (Lake District (England); UF Lakeland (England), Lakes (England))

3.3.51.

008		y y m m d d n a . a c n n d a a b n . . . . a . a a a . . . . . d
040		≠a ____ ≠c ____
151	0	≠a Mexico, Gulf of.
451	0	≠a Gulf of Mexico.
550	0	≠a Bays ≠z Mexico.
550	0	≠a Bays ≠z United States.
670		≠a Lockout, Clyde. The Gulf of Mexico, 1973.
670		≠a *LCSH*, 20th ed. (1997), v. 3, p. 3499 (Mexico, Gulf of; UF Gulf of Mexico; BT Bays--Mexico, Bays--United States) ; v. 1, p. 508 Bays (May Subd Geog)).

008		y y m m d d n a . a c n n d a a b n . . . . a . a a a . . . . . d
040		≠a ____ ≠c ____
550	0	≠a Bays ≠z Mexico.
551	0	≠a Mexico, Gulf of.
670		≠a Lockout, Clyde. The Gulf of Mexico, 1973.
670		≠a *LCSH*, 20th ed. (1997), v. 1, p. 508 (Bays (May Subd Geog)); v. 3, p. 3499 (Mexico, Gulf of).

008		y y m m d d n a . a c n n d a a b n . . . . a . a a a . . . . . d
040		≠a ____ ≠c ____
550	0	≠a Bays ≠z United States.
551	0	≠a Mexico, Gulf of.
670		≠a Lockout, Clyde. The Gulf of Mexico, 1973.
670		≠a *LCSH*, 20th ed. (1997), v. 1, p. 508 (Bays (May Subd Geog)); v. 3, p. 3499 (Mexico, Gulf of).

3.3.52.

008		y y m m d d n a . a c n n d a a b n . . . . a . a a a . . . . . d
040		≠a ____ ≠c ____
151	0	≠a Mississippi River Valley.
451	0	≠a Mississippi Valley.
670		≠a Halley, B.T. Big Father of Waters, 1989 (Mississippi River, Mississippi Valley).
670		≠a *LCSH*, 20th ed. (1997), v. 3, p. 3563 (Mississippi River Valley; UF Mississippi Valley).

3.3.53.

008		y y m m d d n a . a c n n d a a b n . . . . a . a a a . . . . . d
040		≠a ____ ≠c ____
151	0	≠a Pontchartrain, Lake (La.)
451	0	≠a Lake Pontchartrain (La.)
550	0	≠a Lakes ≠z Louisiana.

670 ≠a Jones, Billy Bob. Lake Pontchartrain, c1954.
670 ≠a *LCSH*, 20th ed. (1997), v. 3, p. 4356 (Pontchartrain, Lake (La.); UF Lake Pontchartrain (La.); BT Lakes--Louisiana).

008 yymmddna.acnndaabn...........a.aaa.....d
040 ≠a ____ ≠c ____
150 0 ≠a Lakes ≠z Louisiana.
551 0 ≠a Pontchartrain, Lake (La.)
670 ≠a Jones, Billy Bob. Lake Pontchartrain, c1954.
670 ≠a *LCSH*, 20th ed. (1997), v. 3, p. 3051 (Lakes (May Subd Geog)); p. 4356 (Pontchartrain, Lake (La.)).

3.3.54.
008 yymmddna.acnndaabn...........a.aaa.....d
040 ≠a ____ ≠c ____
151 0 ≠a Salmon River, Middle Fork (Idaho)
451 0 ≠a Middle Fork, Salmon River (Idaho)
5500 ≠a Rivers ≠z Idaho.
670 ≠a Zines, Winfred. Middle Fork of the Salmon, c1980.
670 ≠a *LCSH*, 20th ed. (1997) v. 4, p. 4853 (Salmon River, Middle Fork (Idaho); UF Middle Fork, Salmon River (Idaho); BT Rivers--Idaho)).

008 yymmddna.acnndaabn...........a.aaa.....d
040 ≠a ____ ≠c ____
150 0 ≠a Rivers ≠z Idaho.
551 0 ≠a Salmon River, Middle Fork (Idaho)
670 ≠a Zines, Winfred. Middle Fork of the Salmon, c1980.
670 ≠a *LCSH*, 20th ed. (1997) v. 4, p. 4734 (Rivers (May Subd Geog)); p. 4853 (Salmon River, Middle Fork (Idaho)).

Personal Names

3.3.55.
008 yymmddna.acnndaabn...........a.aaa.....d
040 ≠a ____ ≠c ____
100 1 0 ≠a W, Mickey.
400 1 0 ≠a Jones, Michael.
400 1 0 ≠a Mullins, Al.
670 ≠a Encyclopedic dictionary of African-Americans, c1975. ≠b (Mickey W., born 1/1/42, d. 2/2/70; b. as Michael Jones; also known as Big Al Mullins).

3.3.56.
008 yymmddna.acnndaabn...........a.aaa.....d
040 ≠a ____ ≠c ____
100 1 0 ≠a Davis, Jimmie, ≠d 1902-

400 1 0 ≠a Davis, James Houston, ≠d 1902-
510 1 0 ≠a Louisiana. ≠b Governor (1944-1948 : Davis)
510 1 0 ≠a Louisiana. ≠b Governor (1960-1964 : Davis)
670 ≠a His Louisiana, here I come!, 1963 (Jimmie Davis)
670 ≠a His You are my sunshine, 1985 (James Houston Davis; b. 9/11/1902; governor of Louisiana 1944-48, 1960-64).
678 ≠a Preferred to be known as Jimmie.

008 y y m m d d n a . a c n n d a a b n . . . . a . a a a . . . . . d
040 ≠a ____ ≠c ____
110 1 0 ≠a Louisiana. ≠b Governor (1944-1948 : Davis)
510 1 0 ≠a Louisiana. ≠b Governor (1960-1964 : Davis)
500 1 0 ≠a Davis, Jimmie, ≠d 1902-
670 ≠a His Louisiana, here I come!, 1963 (Jimmie Davis)
670 ≠a His You are my sunshine, 1985 (James Houston Davis; b. 9/11/1902; governor of Louisiana 1944-48, 1960-64).
678 ≠a Preferred to be known as Jimmie.

008 y y m m d d n a . a c n n d a a b n . . . . a . a a a . . . . . d
040 ≠a ____ ≠c ____
110 1 0 ≠a Louisiana. ≠b Governor (1960-1964 : Davis)
510 1 0 ≠a Louisiana. ≠b Governor (1944-1948 : Davis)
500 1 0 ≠a Davis, Jimmie, ≠d 1902-
670 ≠a His Louisiana, here I come!, 1963 (Jimmie Davis)
670 ≠a His You are my sunshine, 1985 (James Houston Davis; b. 9/11/1902; governor of Louisiana 1944-48, 1960-64).
678 ≠a Preferred to be known as Jimmie.

3.3.57.

008 y y m m d d n a . a c n n d a a b n . . . . a . a a a . . . . . d
040 ≠a ____ ≠c ____
100 1 0 ≠a Huey, John, ≠d 1874-1969.
400 1 0 ≠a Smith, Charles John Huey, ≠d 1874-1969.
500 1 0 ≠a Smith, Charles, ≠d 1874-1969.
670 ≠a His The extraneous murders, c1923. ≠b t.p. (John Huey).
670 ≠a Contemptuous authors, v. 1195 (b. 3/29/1874, d. 8/28/1969; b. as Charles John Huey Smith; also wrote as Charles Smith)

008 y y m m d d n a . a c n n d a a b n . . . . a . a a a . . . . . d
040 ≠a ____ ≠c ____
100 1 0 ≠a Smith, Charles, ≠d 1874-1969.
400 1 0 ≠a Smith, Charles John Huey, ≠d 1874-1969.
500 1 0 ≠a Huey, John, ≠d 1874-1969.
670 ≠a His The extraneous murders, c1923. ≠b t.p. (Charles Smith)

670 ≠a Contemptuous authors, v. 1195 (b. 3/29/1874, d. 8/28/1969; b. as Charles John Huey Smith; also wrote as John Huey)

3.3.58.

008 y y m m d d n a . a c n n d a a b n . . . . a . a a a . . . . . d
040 ≠a ____ ≠c ____
100 1 0 ≠a Gogh, Vincent van, ≠d 1853-1890.
400 1 0 ≠a Van Gogh, Vincent, ≠d 1853-1890.
400 1 0 ≠a Gogh, Vincent-Willem van, ≠d 1853-1890.
670 ≠a His Tableaux, aquarelles, dessin..., 1904.
670 ≠a Vincent van Gogh (1853-1890), 1958: (Vincent-Willem van Gogh, b. 3/30/1853; d. 7/29/1890).

3.3.59.

008 y y m m d d n a . a c n n d a a b n . . . . a . a a a . . . . . d
040 ≠a ____ ≠c ____
100 1 0 ≠a Lambert-Pitcherly, Carolyn.
400 1 0 ≠a Pitcherly, Carolyn Lambert.
670 ≠a Her First you must make the roux, c1991 (Carolyn Lambert-Pitcherly)
670 ≠a Great chefs of the South, 1995 (Carolyn Lambert Pitcherly)

3.3.60.

008 y y m m d d n a . a c n n d a a b n . . . . a . a a a . . . . . d
040 ≠a ____ ≠c ____
100 1 0 ≠a Bentley, Susan L.
400 1 0 ≠a Bentley, Sue.
670 ≠a Her Avoyelles Parish, the happy parish, c1979 (Susan L. Bentley)
670 ≠a Lewis, M.L. III Coushatta and the Indians, c1994 (Sue Bentley).

3.3.61.

008 y y m m d d n a . a c n n d a a b n . . . . a . a a a . . . . . d
040 ≠a ____ ≠c ____
100 1 0 ≠a Bartholomew, Don, ≠d 1963-
400 1 0 ≠a Bartholomew, Donald Henry, ≠d 1963-
670 ≠a Don Bartholomew's Mongolia, c1996.
670 ≠a Phone call to author, 5/16/96: full name is Donald Henry Bartholomew; born in Ulaanbaatar, Mongolia, on 1/25/63; usage: Don Bartholomew).

3.3.62.

008 y y m m d d n a . a c n n d a a b n . . . . a . a a a . . . . . d
040 ≠a ____ ≠c ____
100 1 0 ≠a Ward, Humphry, ≠c Mrs., ≠d 1851-1920.
400 1 0 ≠a Ward, Mary Augusta Arnold, ≠d 1851-1920.
400 1 0 ≠a Arnold, Mary Augusta, ≠d 1851-1920.

670 ≠a Her Helbeck of Bannisdale, 1883 (Mrs. Humphry Ward, b. Mary Augusta Arnold; in Hobart, Tasmania, 1851)
670 ≠a Oxford companion to English literature, 1985 (Mary Augusta Ward; d. 1920)
678 ≠a Native of Hobart, Tasmania.

Topical Subject Headings

3.3.63.

008 y y m m d d n a . a c n n d a a b n . . . . a . a a a . . . . . d
040 ≠a ____ ≠c ____
150 0 ≠a Heraldry.
450 0 ≠a Coats of arms.
450 0 ≠a Blazonry.
450 0 ≠a Arms, Coats of.
670 ≠a Brault, G. J. Early blazon, c1972.
670 ≠a *LCSH*, 20th ed. (1997), v. 2, p. 2443 (Heraldry; UF Arms, Coats of, Blazonry, Coats of arms).

3.3.64.

008 y y m m d d n a . a c n n d a a b n . . . . a . a a a . . . . . d
040 ≠a ____ ≠c ____
150 0 ≠a Hounds.
450 0 ≠a Catahoula hounds.
450 0 ≠a Catahoula hog dog.
670 ≠a Jenkins, Huey. Encyclopedia of the Catahoula hound, c1992.
670 ≠a Brown, W.C. The Catahoula hog dog, 1962.
670 ≠a *LCSH*, 20th ed. (1997), v. 2, p. 2537 (Hounds).

3.3.65.

008 y y m m d d n a . a c n n d a a b n . . . . a . a a a . . . . . d
040 ≠a ____ ≠c ____
150 0 ≠a Mental fatigue.
450 0 ≠a Exhaustion, Mental.
450 0 ≠a Fatigue, Mental.
450 0 ≠a Mental overwork.
670 ≠a Green, W.J. Fatigue free, c1992.
670 ≠a Ferguson, Bobby. How to catalog with joy, c1999.

3.3.66.

008 y y m m d d n a . a c n n d a a b n . . . . a . a a a . . . . . d
040 ≠a ____ ≠c ____
150 0 ≠a Rose culture.
450 0 ≠a Rose growing.
670 ≠a Baker, M.L. Roses and their culture, c1991.
670 ≠a *LCSH*, 20th ed. (1997), v. 4, p. 4788 (Rose culture; UF Rose growing)

3.3.67.

008		y y m m d d n a . a c n n d a a b n . . . . a . a a a . . . . . d
040		≠a≠c_
150	0	≠a Rhodesian ridgeback.
450	0	≠a Ridgeback, Rhodesian.
450	0	≠a African lion hound.
450	0	≠a Lion hound, African.
550	0	≠a Hounds.
670		≠a Linzy, J. Rhodesian ridgeback champions, 1955-1980, c1981.
670		≠a *LCSH*, 20th ed. (1997), v. 4, p. 4707 (Rhodesian ridgeback; UF African lion hound; Lion hound, African; Ridgeback, Rhodesian; BT Hounds)

008		y y m m d d n a . a c n n d a a b n . . . . a . a a a . . . . . d
040		≠a ____ ≠c ____
150	0	≠a Hounds.
550	0	≠a Rhodesian ridgeback.
670		≠a Sewell, Joseph T. Hounds of the world, c1975.
670		≠a *LCSH*, 20th ed. (1997), v. 2, p. 2537 (Hounds)

3.3.68.

008		y y m m d d n a . a c n n d a a b n . . . . a . a a a . . . . . d
040		≠a ____ ≠c ____
150	0	≠a Theology.
450	0	≠a Christian theology.
450	0	≠a Theology, Christian.
550	0	≠a Theology, Doctrinal.
550	0	≠a Theology, Practical.
670		≠a Montefiore, H. Credible Christianity, c1994.
670		≠a *LCSH*, 20th ed. (1997), v. 4, p 5548 (Theology; UF Christian theology; Theology, Christian; NT Theology, Doctrinal; Theology, Practical).

008		y y m m d d n a . a c n n d a a b n . . . . a . a a a . . . . . d
040		≠a ____ ≠c ____
150	0	≠a Theology, Doctrinal.
550	0	≠a Theology.
550	0	≠a Theology, Practical.
670		≠a Montefiore, H. Credible Christianity, c1994.
670		≠a *LCSH*, 20th ed. (1997), v. 4, p 5548 (Theology; UF Christian theology; Theology, Christian; NT Theology, Doctrinal; Theology, Practical).

008		y y m m d d n a . a c n n d a a b n . . . . a . a a a . . . . . d
040		≠a ____ ≠c ____
150	0	≠a Theology, Practical.
550	0	≠a Theology, Doctrinal.

550	0	≠a Theology.
670		≠a Montefiore, H. Credible Christianity, c1994.
670		≠a *LCSH*, 20th ed. (1997), v. 4, p 5548 (Theology; UF Christian theology; Theology, Christian; NT Theology, Doctrinal; Theology, Practical).

3.3.69.

008		y y m m d d n a . a c n n d a a b n . . . . a . a a a . . . . . d
040		≠a ____ ≠c ____
150	0	≠a Wreaths.
450	0	≠a Garlands.
550	0	≠a Handicraft.
670		≠a Pflumm, C.C. Hearthstrings, c1993.
670		≠a *LCSH*, 20th ed. (1997), v. 4, p. 6096 (Wreaths; UF Garlands; BT Handicraft).

008		y y m m d d n a . a c n n d a a b n . . . . a . a a a . . . . . d
040		≠a ____ ≠c ____
150	0	≠a Handicraft.
550	0	≠a Wreaths.
670		≠a Pflumm, C.C. Hearthstrings, c1993.
670		≠a *LCSH*, 20th ed. (1997), v. 2, p. 2377 (Handicraft); v. 4, p. 6096 (Wreaths).

3.3.70.

008		y y m m d d n a . a c n n d a a b n . . . . a . a a a . . . . . d
040		≠a ____ ≠c ____
150	0	≠a Acrylic painting.
450	0	≠a Polymer painting.
450	0	≠a Synthetic painting.
670		≠a Taubes, F. Acrylic painting for the beginner, c1971.
670		≠a *LCSH*, 20th ed. (1997), v. 1, p. 34 (Acrylic painting; UF Polymer painting, Synthetic painting).